Instruments around the world

Andy Jackson

Quena – *flute from the Andes*	*4*
Koto – *zither from Japan*	*10*
Atumpan – *'talking' drum from Ghana*	*16*
Duda – *bagpipe from Hungary*	*20*
Didjeridu – *trumpet from Australia*	*26*
Sitar – *lute from North India*	*30*
Gender – *metal xylophone from Indonesia*	*36*
Mbira – *linguaphone from Zimbabwe*	*42*
Sheng – *mouth organ from China*	*46*
Peyote water drum – *kettledrum from North America*	*52*
Hardanger fiddle – *folk violin from Norway*	*56*
Around the world in 80 bars	*62*

Longman

Longman Group UK Limited,
Longman House, Burnt Mill, Harlow,
Essex CM20 2JE, England
and Associated Companies throughout the world.

© Longman Group UK Limited 1988
All rights reserved; no part of this publication
may be reproduced, stored in a retrieval system,
or transmitted in any form or by any means, electronic,
mechanical, photocopying, recording, or otherwise,
without the prior written permission of the Publishers.

First published 1988

ISBN 0 582 22440 3

Set in 10/12 point Times (Linotron)
Produced by Longman Group (F.E.) Limited
Printed in Hong Kong

To Wilfrid Mellers and John Paynter

Acknowledgements

We are grateful to the following for permission to reproduce copyright material:

Boosey & Hawkes Music Publishers Limited for an extract from 'The Prince of the Pagodas' by Benjamin Britten © Copyright 1957 by Hawkes & Son (London) Ltd; Faber Music Limited, London for extracts from 'Curlew River' by Benjamin Britten © 1964, 1965 Faber Music Ltd; Chadwick Nomis Limited for an extract from 'Canton' by David Sylvian and Stephen Jansen; Peters Edition Limited, London for an extract from 'Music of Changes' by John Cage Copyright © 1961 by Henmar Press Inc., New York; SBK Songs Limited for the song 'Within You Without You' by George Harrison © 1967 Northern Songs, under licence to SBK Songs for the world; Universal Edition (London) Limited for an extract from 'Music for Strings, Percussion and Celesta' by Béla Bartók.

The copyright work 'The Prince of the Pagodas' by Benjamin Britten is specifically excluded from any blanket photocopying arrangements.

We are grateful to the following for permission to reproduce photographs: Promotion Australia, London, page 26 below; Barnabys Picture Library, page 6, 28 (photo: Bill Angove), 29 (photo: Hubertus Kanus); Bartók Archives, Budapest, page 22 below; Stephen Benson, page 26 above; The British Library, page 13; Camera Press, page 48 below left (photo: Horst Tappe); P. R. Cooke, page 42, 59; G. D. Hackett, page 33, 39; The High Commission of India, page 30; Japan Information Centre, page 12 below; Edward C. Van Ness, page 36; Northern Illinois School of Music, page 49 (photo: George Tarbay); Peters Edition, page 48 below right; The Photo Source, page 20; Popperfoto, page 10, 12 above, 16, 22 above, 38 above; Royal Norwegian Embassy, page 58; Dr Bálint Sárosi, page 23; School of Scottish Studies, page 46; South American Pictures, page 4, 7; Topham Picture Library, page 32; *UNESCO* Courier, page 55; University of Exeter, page 52 (photo: Edward S. Curtis); Virgin Records, page 38 below, 48 above centre. We are unable to trace the copyright holder of the photograph on page 18; 56 and would be grateful for any information that would enable us to do so.

Cover: Men playing carved wooden flutes, Tropix.

Illustrated by Caroline Ewan and Oxford Illustrators

A note to teachers

Each section of this book deals with one instrument and the culture to which it belongs. The sections are completely self-contained and can be used in isolation.

The practical element of each section begins with simple experiments with sound, builds up into more complicated playing exercises involving a high degree of group cooperation and ends with a structured composition. If you bring a few of these pieces to performance standard, you could then have a go at the final piece, 'Around the world in 80 bars', which links pieces together by means of sounds representing different modes of transport.

The most ambitious practical activity is making working copies of the original instruments from everyday materials, mainly household waste. Making these is not essential to the success of any of the sections, but it can be a lot of fun, and some of them are really quite easy. The important thing is to have all the materials and tools to hand. So start collecting early; it can take a long time to collect enough toilet roll innards to make 30 didjeridus!

Do not expect perfect sound production first time, it is important to experiment, make mistakes and learn why and how each instrument makes the sound that it does. Also, the instruments will disintegrate very quickly. If you want more durable items, make them in the same way, but use wood instead of cardboard, glue instead of sellotape, putty instead of Blu-tack, and so on.

If you would like to see instruments from other cultures in their original state, there may be some in the ethnographic section of your local museum, and there are several excellent collections in the London museums and at the larger universities. If you would like more information about any of the instruments and their music, start with the relevant country in *The New Grove Dictionary of Music and Musicians*. These articles are aimed at adults and I am afraid I do not know of any comprehensive work on ethnic music suitable for children.

I have tried to keep the listening material confined to pieces to which most music teachers have access. This has meant concentrating on Western music, but your record library may well have some discs of music from further afield and several record companies such as Lyrichord, Nonesuch and Bärenreiter-Musicaphon (who publish the UNESCO collection), have excellent lists of ethnic and folk music.

These pages try to give glimpses into music-making in different parts of the world. Some of the things mentioned will seem similar to aspects of our own music, others may seem alien, or funny. It is tempting to assume that Western music is 'better' than, say, Australian aboriginal music because it has greater range, uses more instruments, has a system of notation, or simply because it 'sounds nicer'. But each is a complex system in its own right, adequate for the requirements of the society that uses it and continually developing to meet new requirements. Neither is 'better' than the other, they are just different manifestations of something we call music.

In an increasingly multi-racial society, it is important that we respect the musical cultures of other nations and learn from them. One of the things I have learned from looking into music worldwide is that it need not be a commodity produced by a few skilled practitioners to be consumed by the rest of the population. The exercises in this book try to give everyone, regardless of their previous training in music, the chance to participate creatively as players and listeners and to contribute towards the production of pieces which largely depend for their success on the enthusiasm of those taking part.

Andy Jackson

QUENA

Flute from the Andes

The South American Andes mountains cover large areas of Ecuador, Peru, Bolivia and Chile. Throughout this region, the most popular instrument is a flute known as the quena, (pronounced *ken-a*).

It is an instrument with a very long history. In the past, quenas were made out of clay, metal or human bones. Andean Indians believed that playing flutes made from the bones of your enemies gave you power over them. It was also played as a sign of mourning. An Inca legend tells of how the sister-wife of an Inca king, who had been killed in battle, went into his tomb, made a flute from his shin bone and played a sad melody on it.

This is a very unusual story because it features a woman playing the quena. In South America and many other parts of the world, flute playing is considered unsuitable for women because of the instrument's obviously male shape.

After the defeat of the Inca civilization by the Spaniard Francisco Pizarro in 1533, Christian missionaries were horrified by the superstitions associated with instruments made from human bones and did everything in their power to replace the native music with their own religious and folk music. One 17th century missionary boasted of having personally destroyed 4,623 drums and flutes in Peruvian villages, and in 1614 a law was passed which made the possession of such 'pagan' objects a serious offence. The punishment was 300 lashes in the public square.

Some people still have this attitude towards traditional Andean music, but in spite of hundreds of years of persecution, the quena is still with us, though now it is more likely to be made of bamboo or plastic piping. Bones are still used but they will probably come from an animal such as a llama.

Things to do

1. Take any tube, a pen top or empty pen casing will do. If it is open at both ends, close off one end with a finger.

Now blow across the top of the tube until you can make a clear, flute-like note. This is not always easy and can take some time to perfect. It sometimes helps if you slightly curl your bottom lip against the edge of the tube.

2. Look at the map and pictures on page 5. Describe the different ways in which people hold flutes in different countries. How is the quena held? Is it like a fife or more like a recorder?

Flutes throughout the world

Side-blown flutes such as the familiar orchestral flute and piccolo are found in most parts of the world. Fifes such as this one played by a boy soldier from the American War of Independence are a variety of side-blown flute which have been associated with military and processional music since the 16th century.

The tin whistle is a popular folk instrument throughout much of the British Isles, particularly in Ireland. This instrument is sometimes called the penny whistle on account of its cheapness. It uses a mouthpiece to direct the player's breath against a sharp-edged hole in the metal tube.

The recorder is a very ancient instrument which fell into disuse during the 18th century. In 1919 a Swiss instrument maker called Arnold Dolmetsch began a revival of recorder playing and today it is the best known of all wind instruments.

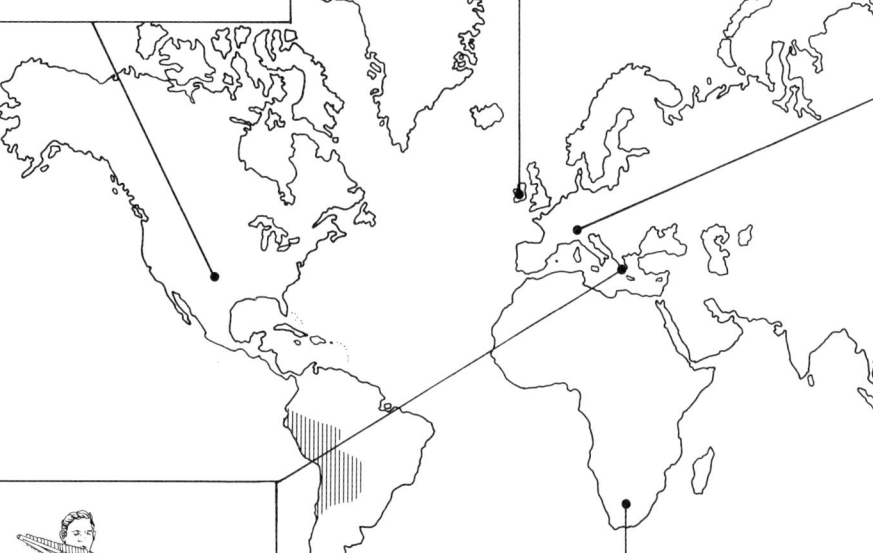

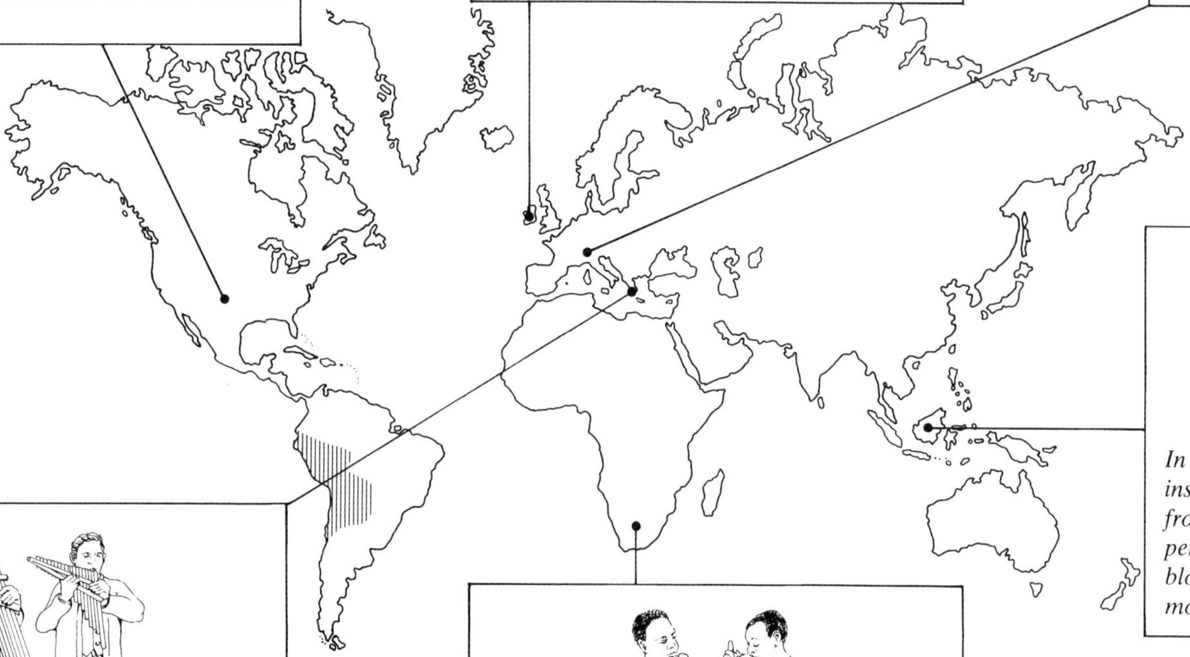

Panpipes are sets of tubes of varying lengths. When you blow across the top of the tubes, each one plays a different note, and melodies can be put together by moving from one tube to another. Although panpipes are named after the Greek god Pan, they can be found in most parts of the world.

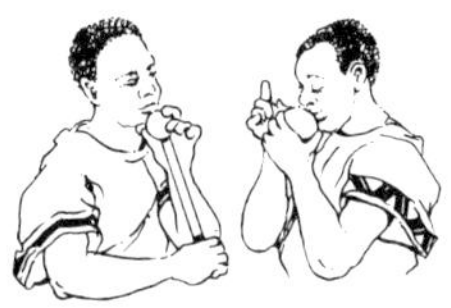

The South African shiwaya is made from the hollowed-out shell of a fruit. This type of instrument is called a vessel flute because its body tends to be round rather than long and thin. In Europe, the best-known type of vessel flute is the toy ocarina.

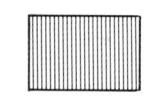

In Borneo the nose flute is the 'national' instrument. People there believe that breath from the nose has special power, so they have perfected a technique of playing the flute by blowing through the nose rather than the mouth.

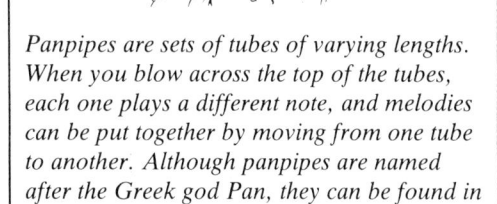

= area covered by the quena

Listening

South American folk music has been used as the basis for pieces by many composers. The best-known are Victor Chavez's *Sinfonia Indica*, Aaron Copland's *Three Latin American Sketches*, and several pieces by the Brazilian composer Hietor Villa-Lobos.

The influence in these works comes from Brazil and Mexico. Compositions by Peruvians such as André Sas and the Indian Teodoro Valcarcel are not often heard outside South America. But there is one piece of Andean folk music which has become very famous indeed.

In 1970 the American songwriter Paul Simon took a beautiful Peruvian melody and added some words in English. When Paul Simon and Art Garfunkel recorded *El Condor Passa* it was an instant success.

The words to this song are like a jigsaw puzzle, piecing together a picture of a man 'tied to the ground' who wishes he were a bird and dreams of flying away and escaping the sadness of his life. The song is accompanied by the quena, which does give it a very sad sound.

El Condor Passa

You may be able to hear traditional Andean music in Britain because there are several groups of South American musicians living here who give regular concerts. These people are forced to live away from their own countries, because they disagree with the political system there and would be persecuted if they played their music in public. So they live and play in Europe, keeping alive the traditional music of their homes and trying to win support for their political beliefs.

Simon and Garfunkel in concert

Learning to play the quena

Music was treated with great respect by the Incas who needed it for their religious rituals. There was a School of Music at Cuzco as early as 1350 A.D. and skilled musicians were brought from foreign countries to play there.

But after the collapse of the Inca empire, organized native music disappeared or combined with European music to make a new type of folk music. Some of the old Inca music became the property of Indian tribes, often living in remote places far away from persecution by the Spanish invaders.

These tribes had no formal musical education. Many of them did not even have a word in their language meaning 'music'. Because music was always associated with dance or some other activity and never took place by itself, there was no need for it to have a separate name. Learning to play an instrument was a matter of copying other players. Andean Indians have developed ways of making music without having to be very skilful on an instrument.

Hocket

South American flutes are often played in groups. Each player in the group has only one note to play, but by playing it at the correct time, that note becomes part of a whole melody.

Bolivian panpipes played in a group to the accompaniment of drums

This method of playing is not confined to South America. European campanology (bell-ringing) works in a very similar way. It is known as hocket technique and players often dance at the same time as they play.

Playing exercises

1. Play the pen tops, etc. which you used earlier in the chapter. Listen hard to the note your 'flute' plays. Form yourselves into groups of five or six people whose notes are all different.

Stand in a line with the lowest notes at one end and the highest notes at the other. This will probably mean that the longest 'flutes' will be at one end of the line and the shortest at the other, but it may not be as simple as that, so do listen to the sound your instruments make.

Give each flute a number. Call the lowest note number 1, the one next to it 2 and so on.

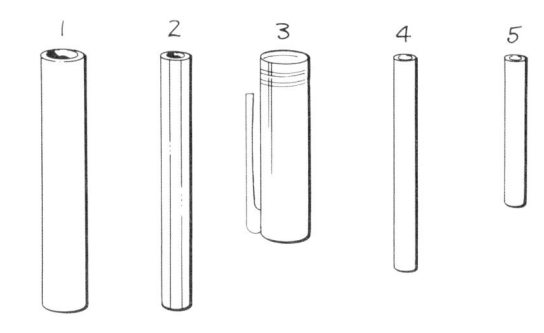

Now play a tune using these notes. Write out a series of numbers. The person with the first number plays a note. Everyone prepares to blow when their number is next in line, and plays as soon as the previous note ends. At first, it is best to play fairly slowly with every note lasting for the same length of time, but as you begin to respond more quickly to the other members of the group, try altering the length of notes to make more interesting rhythms.

2. If anyone can play the recorder, play the two tunes given so far. To make it sound like a quena, make a wavering sound on each note by repeatedly catching your breath in your throat as quickly as possible. Guitarists or pianists can add the chords written above the tunes.

In modern Andean music, quenas are often substituted by other instruments and a guitar accompaniment is usual, so you could be producing a very authentic sound.

Making a quena

There are some differences between the quena played today and that played by the Incas. For instance, modern quenas have more finger holes so that they can play melodies influenced by European music more easily. But the basic form of the instrument, a simple tube with holes in it and a notch at one end for blowing into has remained unchanged for thousands of years.

YOU WILL NEED
2 Smartie tubes or tubes of similar size
A sharp knife
Sellotape

HOW TO MAKE Time needed 5 minutes
Knock the bottom out of both tubes and sellotape them together to form a continuous tube. Then cut a small V-shaped notch in one end of the tube.

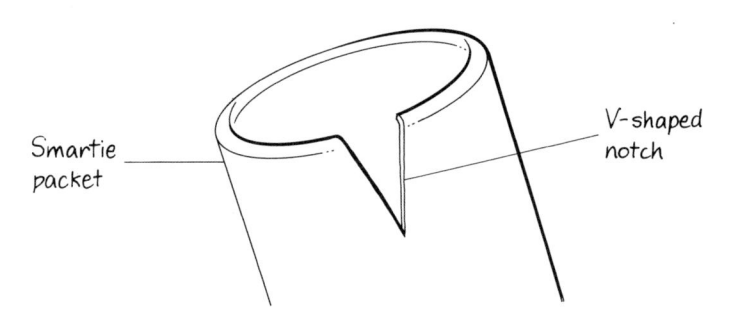

At the other end of the tube, cut 5 or 6 holes. Make them small at first.

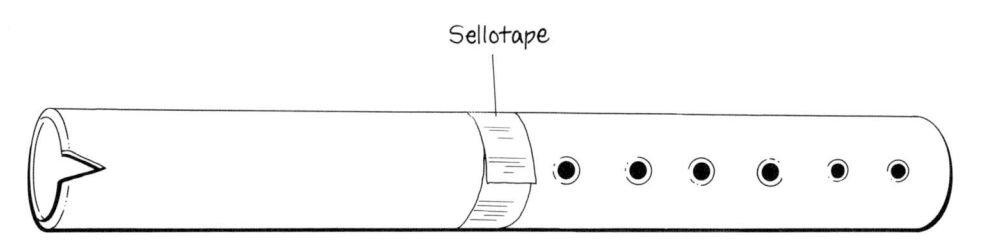

Playing your quena

You have already experimented with producing sounds from closed-ended tubes, now you have to make an open-ended tube 'speak'. The sound actually comes from blowing into the notch at the top of the flute. Press your lower lip against the outside edge of the tube opposite the notch. It will look something like this:

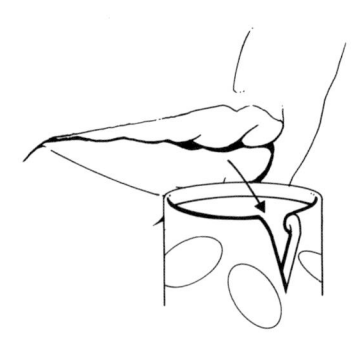

Shape the upper lip so that a jet of air is directed down into the notch. You may need to blow very hard initially to produce a full tone, but should be able to ease off once you have learned exactly where to blow. If the tone will not quite come, you may need to cut the notch a little deeper.

Once you are producing a steady tone, put your fingers one by one over the holes in the lower end of the flute, starting with the one nearest to your mouth. As you increase the number of fingers, the pitch of the note you are playing will become lower.

Once you are used to playing these other notes, you may feel that you want to alter the pitch of some of them to play a particular type of melody. Cutting a larger hole will make the note higher. If you want to make a note lower or completely alter the pitch, simply sellotape over the hole and cut another one.

Playing: Baile del Inca

This piece describes how the music of the Incas (played on a variety of flutes) was destroyed by the Spanish invaders (guitars and drums). But the two types of music eventually join together to form a new sound.

The title means 'Dance of the Inca'. This is a Peruvian dance which acts out the death of Atahualpa, the Inca king. Some of you could dance or mime to the music if you wish.

Preparation

Split into four groups and practise your parts.

GROUP 1   Guitars and drums

Play in one rhythm throughout.

To start off with, guitars strum this rhythm on the open strings, but in the last section (J) they play individual strings.

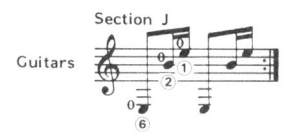

Play louder as the V-shape gets wider.

GROUP 2   Recorders and flutes

Learn to play this melody. Don't forget the wavering tone.

GROUP 3   Pen tops, etc.

Play from the highest to the lowest note in hocket using this rhythm:

The speed is indicated by the zig-zag line. The closer the lines, the faster you play.

GROUP 4   Quenas

Each player finds a note which fits in well with the tune played by group 2. Small dots tell you to play quietly, larger dots mean play more loudly. If the dots are close together play fast, if they are further apart play more slowly.

To play

Each section last 10 seconds. Because you do not need to come in or end at any exact point, you do not need a conductor, just look at a clock or count up to 10 slowly.

Any of the sections can be repeated. You must agree on which ones before you start playing.

The final section lasts for however long it takes group 2 to play the whole of their melody, and is repeated many times.

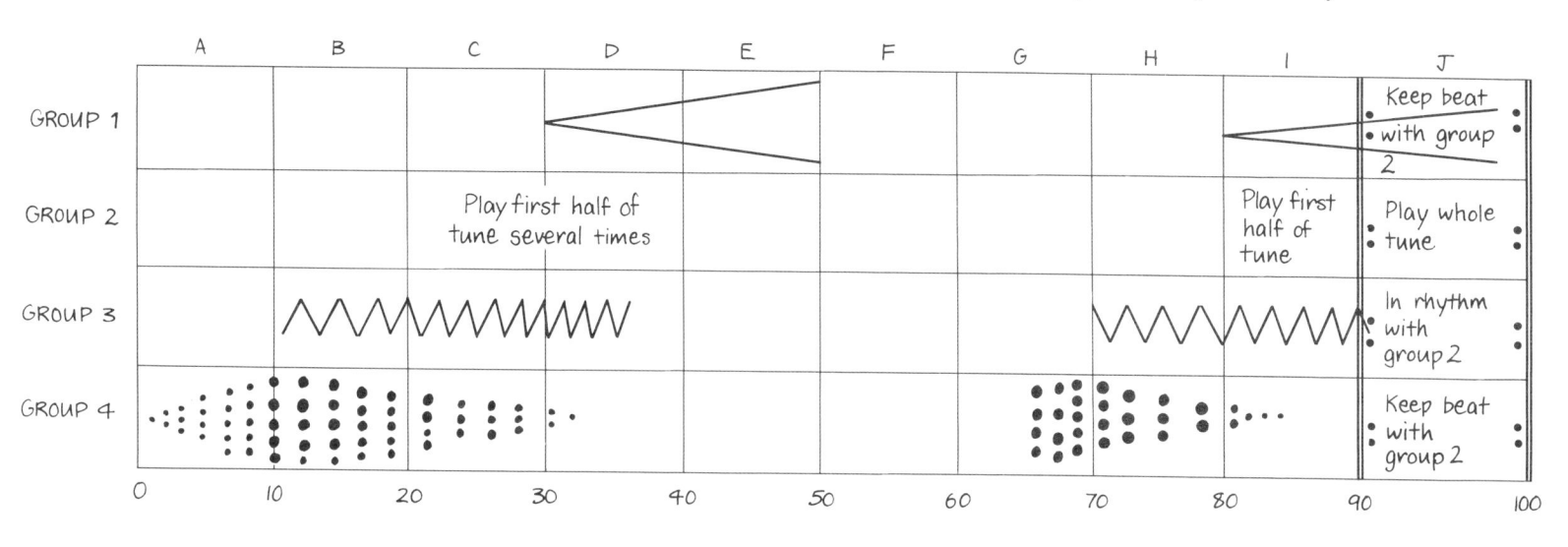

KOTO

Zither from Japan

Zithers are instruments which produce a sound by vibrating a string stretched over some sort of resonator.

The koto is nowadays the most widely played Japanese instrument. It is particularly popular with young ladies, who think that they are more likely to find a husband if they have artistic accomplishments. It is played in the home and in concerts, solo and in groups. In fact, it has a position rather like our piano in that it can both play melodies and accompany singers or other instruments, and every musical household would be expected to have one.

To understand why the koto has this position in Japanese musical life, it is necessary to know something of its history.

There is a famous 11th century story about a prince called Genji who fell in love with a young lady because of the beauty of her koto playing before he had even seen her! When Genji had to leave the lady to return to affairs of state, he left his own instrument with her and promised to be 'as constant as the middle string of the koto', which is always tuned the same.

Later on, in the Edo period of Japanese history (1615–1868), Tokyo was full of young women from wealthy provincial families. They were there as political hostages. The idea was that their influential relatives would be unlikely to cause trouble in case their daughters were harmed. This system meant that there were a lot of wealthy but bored women who turned to music as a way of passing the time.

Here is a typical koto song dealing with the sort of subject thought suitable for young ladies. Translated, it means:

Cherry blossoms in the sky in March, All the view like mist and clouds, Blowing with fragrance.

Sakura Sakura

Sa-ku-ra sa-ku-ra, Ya-yo-i no so-ra—wa mi-wa-ta-su ka-gi-ri, Ka-su-mi ka ku-mo-ka mi-o-i zo i-za-ru, I-za-yah, I-za-ya mi-ni yu-ka-ro.

When the Emperor began a policy of rapid westernization in 1868 and traditional Japanese music was discouraged as 'old-fashioned', most Japanese instruments fell out of use. But the koto had become so popular that it survived. Consequently, when the Japanese government decided to revive traditional music in the 20th century as a way of promoting the sort of national spirit needed to fight wars against China, Russia and America, the koto became the national instrument.

Things to do

1. Stretch a rubber band around a hardback book. Place a pencil underneath the band in roughly the centre of the book. Pluck the band. The sound will be amplified by the cover of the book.

You have made and played a simple zither. Experiment with the sound, notice how if you move the pencil to the left, the right-hand side of the band makes a lower sound when plucked and the left-hand side, which is shorter, plays a higher note.

2. Write a story which features an instrument in the action. There are several well-known tales such as the *Pied Piper of Hamelin* or the Walls of Jericho story from the Bible which could give you some ideas, as well as the tale of Prince Genji.

Zithers throughout the world

One of the characteristic instrumental sounds from Eastern Europe is the cimbalom. The strings are hit with padded hammers to give a rippling effect.

The Indian vina consists of a long stick over which strings are stretched, and two gourd resonators. It is dedicated to the goddess of wisdom, Sarasvati, and is the most highly respected of all Indian instruments.

This komungo from Korea is similar to the koto, but it has wooden frets instead of bridges and is played with a piece of wood, not with the fingers.

The European harpsichord was the main keyboard instrument in the 17th and 18th centuries. It is a type of zither because it consists of strings stretched over a soundboard. These are played by small quills which pluck the strings when a key is pressed down. The modern piano is also a zither in which the strings are hit by felt hammers.

The valiha is a zither from Malagasy which uses a tube of wood as a soundbox. Copper strings are attached to the tube and raised over small bridges.

Trough zithers are an instrument found only in the area around Uganda in central Africa. A long string is laced over a shallow bowl and plucked or brushed to produce a sound. Among the Bahaya people of Tanzania it is an honoured instrument played by professional musicians for the entertainment of chiefs.

= area covered by the koto

Listening

Benjamin Britten (1913–1976) was an English composer who was interested in the music of other countries. In 1956 he went on a world tour which took him to many Far Eastern countries including Japan.

Britten was especially impressed by the Japanese Noh plays, in which the actors wear huge masks and move very slowly. They are accompanied by music played by a small group of instruments which use notes sparingly. The overall effect is of powerful emotions being restrained by a rigid style of drama.

When he returned to England, Britten wrote a piece of dramatic music called *Curlew River*, which had the same atmosphere as a Noh play. He borrowed the story from Japan and much of the music is based on sounds and techniques used in Japanese music.

Benjamin Britten

A Noh play with musicians onstage

Notice how the harp is used here. It is the Western instrument which sounds most like the koto and it plays a series of notes with wide gaps between them in a strict rhythm. The singer is instructed to sing freely, his notes do not necessarily coincide with the harp accompaniment.

Compare the music above with this Japanese song by Yatsuhashi Kengyo. He was a blind composer who lived in the 17th century and is regarded as the father of modern koto music.

You can see how in this piece also the accompaniment consists of a series of widely-spaced notes with a fairly regular rhythm against which the voice weaves an independent part.

In *Curlew River* other instruments such as the flute and drums are often used to make a Japanese sound. Also, the way the instruments and voices are asked to play together is very unusual in European music. In the given extract you can see how the voice and harp play together at figure 46 but then play at their own speeds. They will not have to play at exactly the same time again until figure 47 which comes about a minute later.

This method of group playing is used in Japan where the cues for coming together are given by the drums. Each player needs to listen very carefully to the overall sound.

Britten's music borrows ideas from Japanese music, but still sounds English. In *Curlew River* he set out to show that music from opposite sides of the earth can be brought together. As the chorus sing in the middle of the piece:

Curlew River, smoothly flowing
Between the lands of East and West,
Dividing person from person.
Ah, Ferryman, row your boat!
Bring nearer, nearer, person to person.

Learning to play the koto

There is a special relationship between teachers and pupils in Japan. A music teacher will expect loyalty and respect from his pupils who will instinctively feel a deep affection towards their 'sensei' (master). The teacher inspires respect because he stands for the continuity of tradition. Tradition is thought of as a good thing because it is the opposite of change. So music teaching stresses playing pieces in exactly the same way as the sensei plays them.

On a given day pupils turn up for tuition on a 'first come first served' basis. Several pupils may be waiting for their lessons at the same time. They sit in an adjoining room and listen to the lesson in progress through the paper walls.

Each lesson consists of playing one piece. The teacher usually plays along with the pupil and there is very little discussion or explanation. The pupil learns by copying the teacher's sounds and movements. This is called learning by rote. Written music is never used except as a way of remembering something which has already been learnt. So every pupil, in theory, turns out to be a carbon copy of his teacher.

Obviously, this system of teaching is very time-consuming and is becoming less popular in modern, progressive Japan. But many musicians still learn in this way because they enjoy the comradeship of the other pupils. They also form strong ties with their teachers and often go on outings and to social gatherings with them.

Playing exercises

1. Try learning a piece in Japanese fashion by rote. Choose a 'master'. This does not have to be a teacher, just someone who can read music accurately.

The master sings or plays the first note of the song given on page 10. Everyone else repeats this note. Only the master looks at the written music. When he/she is satisfied that everyone knows the first note, the master sings the first two notes. These are repeated until everyone can manage them. Then the first three notes are tackled.

You may decide to limit yourselves to learning only a section of the tune but you will get to know it very well, especially the first few notes.

2. You are now going to sing the tune at different speeds. Everyone picks their own speed; if you only feel confident singing the first three notes, then sing them very slowly, but if you can manage the whole tune you will have to go quite fast.

This could be chaotic. But everyone knows what the first few notes of the tune sound like and comes together on these notes every time they are repeated. You need to choose someone to perform the whole tune or section which you have learnt and all listen to him or her carefully.

There will be times when you have finished your part of the tune and are waiting for the lead singer to come round to the 'meeting point' again. You have three choices here:

1. Sing your section again.
2. Hold on to your last note.
3. Clap, then listen quietly for the meeting point.

Everyone claps together at the meeting point.

Japanese artist's depiction of young women playing music

Making a koto

YOU WILL NEED

A plank of wood (as big or small as you like)
10 small screws
5 lengths of nylon string (old guitar strings or fishing line will do) about 10 cm longer than your plank
A piece of thick wire (coat hanger)
5 small blocks of wood or plastic (chess pieces or cotton reels)
Screwdriver
Sellotape

HOW TO MAKE **Time needed 10 minutes**

Fix 5 of the screws into one end of the plank (end A), spacing them evenly and leaving about 1 cm showing. Use sellotape to fix the piece of thick wire to the edge of this end of the plank.

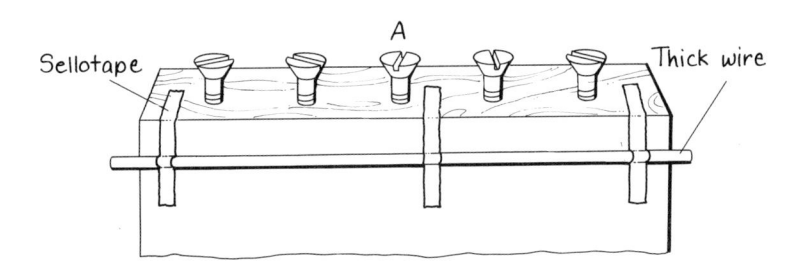

Now fix the other 5 screws into the opposite end of the plank (end B). Make a loop in one of the lengths of string and place it over a screw at this end. Pull the string tight and wrap its other end several times around the facing screw at end A. Finish off with a knot. Repeat this for each of the five strings.

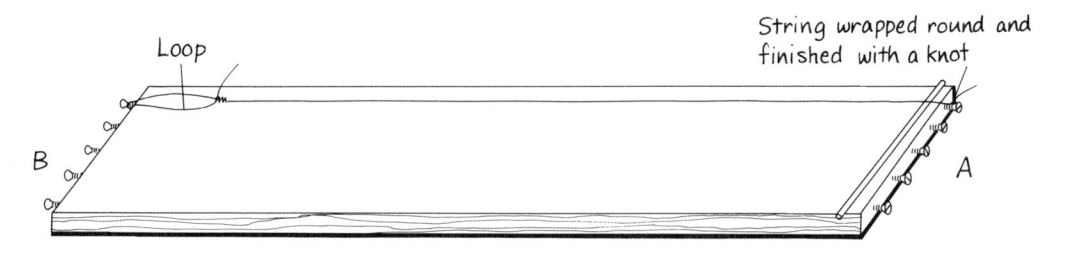

Place the blocks of wood or plastic under the strings to make bridges. This should stretch the strings very tight. Your koto is now ready to play.

Playing your koto

Place your right hand at end A of your koto close to the point where the strings pass over the wire. Pluck a string with a finger. It should produce a pleasant, delicate sound. The volume can be increased by placing the instrument on a table or other large expanse of wood for extra resonance.

Experiment with your koto and see if you can invent some interesting sounds. Here are a couple to get you started:

1. Pluck the string with your right hand, but alter the sound by placing your left hand on the string at the other side of the bridge and pressing. By moving the left hand up and down very quickly, you can produce a sound known as 'tremolo' (trembling).
2. Press the string down with your left hand before you pluck the string with your right hand. Then release it suddenly for an explosive start to a note.

Tuning your koto

The koto must be one of the easiest instruments to tune up. Just move the bridge until the plucked part of the string is the right length to play the note you want.

With five strings, you can tune each string differently and play any melody which uses only five notes, such as *Jingle Bells* or *Go Tell Aunt Nancy*. But it will be much more interesting to tune the strings to a Japanese scale. Ask someone to play these notes (one at a time) on a piano and then find the same notes on the koto by moving the bridges.

If all your strings are at roughly the same tension, the arrangement of the bridges should now look something like this:

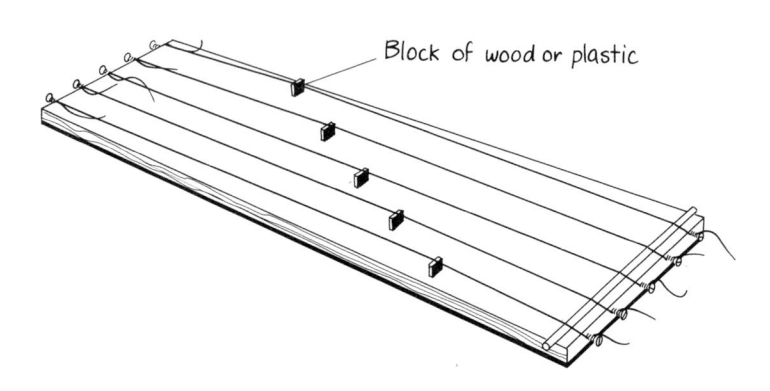

Playing: Hogaku and Seiyogaku

In Japanese, the word hogaku means Japanese music as opposed to seiyogaku which means Western music. This piece uses mainly Western instruments along with a Japanese scale and methods of playing. So it is named after both styles of music.

Preparation
Split into three groups and practise your parts.

GROUP 1 Drums and drum-caller
Use drums and other 'hard' percussion instruments such as sticks and rasps. The first thing this group does is make a large copy of the diagram on this page and pin it on a wall so that it will rotate.

One person does not play an instrument but becomes the drum-caller. It is the drum-caller's job to slowly turn the diagram in an *anti-clockwise* direction. When the words 'Ho' or 'Yo' come to the top, the drum-caller shouts out the word as a warning to the other members of the group to be ready to play. A second or two later, the small black triangle comes to the top and this is a sign for everyone to strike their drums once. Practise listening to the drum-caller very carefully so that you all play at the same time.

Everyone also plays when the large black triangle is at the top, but here it is not necessary to play together; the sounds can be scattered about until the triangle has moved on.

GROUP 2 Kotos
Use Kotos and any other plucked stringed instruments such as guitars, violins and cellos played pizzicato, or the insides of a piano, (mark the correct strings with chalk). This group splits into two sections. Section A learns to play these notes:

Section B plays these notes:

The small black notes are played very quickly, the white notes are held on. Everyone plays at their own speed. If you do not know all the notes on your instrument, just play those which you can manage. Section A plays when the shaded half of the diagram is on top, B when the light half comes up. Keep repeating the notes until it is time for the other section to take over.

GROUP 3 Singers, recorders and violins
Use singers, recorders, violins and any other melody instruments. Choose a 'master' and learn to play the following tunes by rote. Play tune A for the shaded section of the diagram.

Play tune B for the light section of the diagram.

Repeat the tune you are playing until the drum-caller instructs you to change to the other tune.

To play
To start, the drum-caller begins to turn the diagram and groups 2 and 3 play A material. Group 1 will add their percussion to the sound at the large black triangle and again at the small triangle. This 'meeting point' also acts as a sign to groups 1 and 2 to change to their B material.

If the drum-caller listens to the tunes played by group 3, the meeting points can be timed to come at the ends of tunes rather than half-way through them.

To finish, the drum-caller shouts out the cue word twice. At the next small triangle, everyone plays one note and stops.

ATUMPAN

'Talking' drum from Ghana

Throughout Africa there is a close relationship between music and language. This is most obvious in the 'talking' drums used to send messages and to play music which may sound purely instrumental to listeners who do not understand the meaning of the various beats.

There is a Ghanaian legend that during the colonial wars, Ashanti warriors had trapped some British soldiers at the top of a fort. They brought in a pair of atumpan and began to dance to a rhythm based on the words 'Oburoni bewu abansoro'.

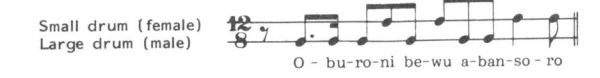

Small drum (female)
Large drum (male)
O - bu-ro-ni be-wu a-ban-so-ro

So the atumpan were used to provide music for dancing, and to send a message at the same time. The soldiers would have been even more terrified if they had understood the message. It means 'The white man will die upstairs'.

Notice how two drums, one high-pitched and one low-pitched, are used to give the meaning of the words. This is because many Africans speak 'tone languages' in which the meaning of a word may depend on its pitch. So it is possible to imitate speech more realistically by using a variety of sounds.

> 'Ever since the Creator created the world,
> The drummer is treated gently and kindly,
> A person becomes a drummer that he may get something to eat.'

This Ashanti proverb tells us a lot about the people who play the atumpan. Firstly, they are important people who are treated well by others. Master drummers in Africa do not just provide entertainment, they are sometimes expected to act as a priest or doctor, or even as a local historian, making up songs telling of their people's past.

Secondly, in return for the responsibility placed on him and for his skill, he is given a living. Many drummers may also farm or have some other way of making money. Few people choose to 'become a drummer', they are more likely to be born into a family which specializes in music.

Things to do

1. Try sending messages by tapping out the rhythm of a sentence, like 'Five minutes to lunch'.

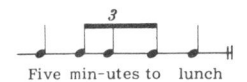

Five min-utes to lunch

Can others understand what you are saying? Your messages will be clearer if you use more than one type of sound for tapping. For instance, you can tap with a pencil in one hand and a rubber in the other, or the nails of one hand and the palm of the other.

Now speak your message and notice how your voice goes up and down. Tap out your message again, this time following the pattern of high and low sounds with different types of tapping.

2. Make up a proverb which expresses your own opinion about musicians. For example, 'Don't leave your money out when there's a pianist about'.

Drums throughout the world

A drum with carved legs from Hawaii. In many areas of the world, drums are shaped to represent parts of the human body.

The Shawnee big drum is sometimes beaten by several players, each holding a single stick.

The drum kit used in jazz, dance and pop music consists of drums of various sizes plus cymbals.

Kakko is a small barrel drum which rests on a stand. It is sometimes used for atmospheric effects in Japanese Kabuki plays.

This huge da-daiko, also from Japan, is suspended in a decorative frame and hit with laquered beaters. It is part of the Gagaku orchestra which plays traditional court music.

In many countries, drums are associated with some type of flute, (think of the fife and drum bands which used to accompany armies into battle). In Bolivia, panpipes are played with a drum which has pieces of wood attached to the rear skin. These rattle when the drum is played in the same way as the snare on a snare drum.

The Indian tabla is a pair of drums used to accompany classical music and singing. The smaller drum is tuned to a definite pitch by using a small hammer, but the larger drum produces a variety of pitches and sliding sounds by being pressed with the heel of the left hand while the fingers produce the rhythm.

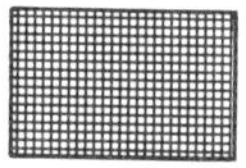

▦ = area covered by the atumpan

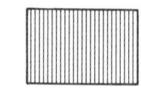

▦ = area in which other types of 'talking drums' are used

Learning to play the atumpan

In Africa, children are involved with music from an early age. As mothers rock their babies to sleep, they sing nonsense songs which imitate drum rhythms. Children are carried on their mother's backs to events where music is played. By the time a child is walking, he (drummers are still always male) may be playing a toy drum.

When he is a little older, the young drummer may be given occasional instruction by an adult. He will not learn from written notation, but will memorize the rhythmic patterns and method of playing them by using spoken syllables. As the trainee musician grows up, he will have to learn and remember hundreds of drumming patterns. By the time he is a teenager, he may be playing a minor part in professional drum ensembles.

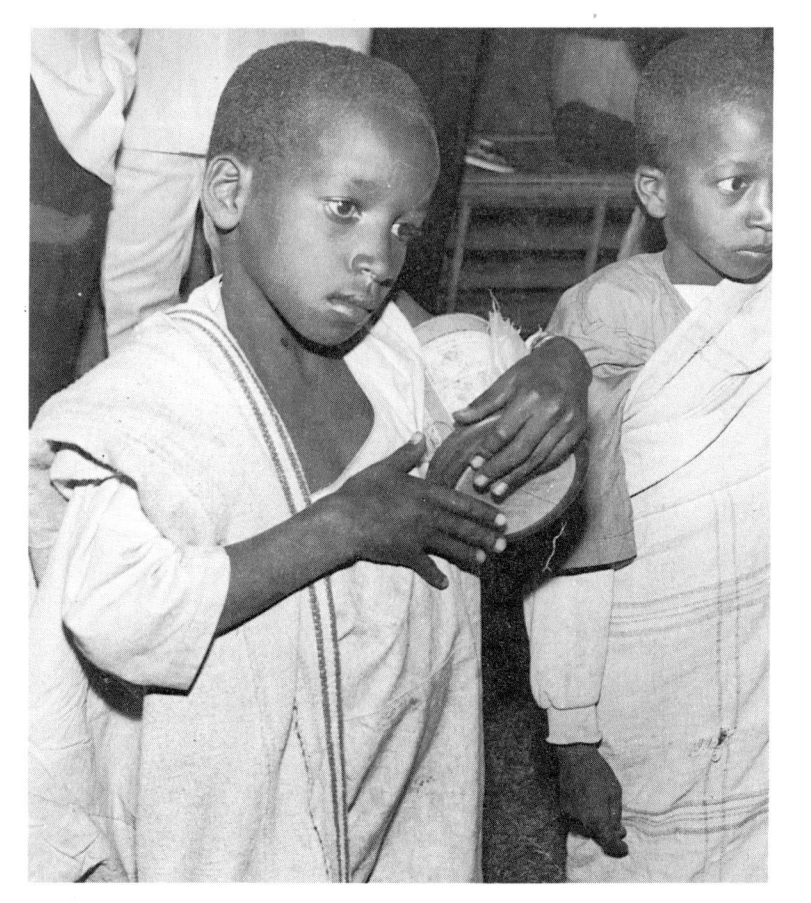

Making an atumpan

YOU WILL NEED
A round container (plastic plant-pot/cardboard cylinder)
Two rods longer than the diameter of the container (knitting needles/piece of dowel)
Plastic bag
Thick wire longer than the circumference of your container (wire coathanger/electrical cable)
Needle and thread
String
Pair of pliers

HOW TO MAKE **Time needed 20 minutes**
Using the pliers, shape the wire into a ring slightly larger than the top of your container and twist the two ends together. Put this ring on the flattened-out plastic bag and cut round it, leaving a 2.5 cm margin. Sew the circle of plastic onto the wire ring as tightly as possible, folding the edges of the plastic over the wire and sewing through both surfaces.

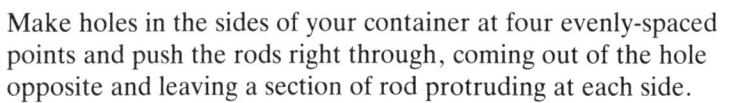

Make holes in the sides of your container at four evenly-spaced points and push the rods right through, coming out of the hole opposite and leaving a section of rod protruding at each side.

Make four evenly-spaced holes in the plastic circle going through both layers of plastic near to the wire. Using a single piece of string, lace the plastic circle onto the container. Pass the string through the plastic from the top, then down and underneath one of the protruding parts of a rod, then up and through the next hole from the top. Tie the string tightly when the two ends meet having passed under all four pieces of rod and all four holes in the plastic.

Playing your atumpan
Hold the drum in one hand by the strings and hit it lightly with the other hand. Bounce the hand off the drum head rather than letting it rest on it. This should give a full, booming sound. If the drum makes a dull thud, it is probably because the drum head is too slack. Remedy this by re-tightening the strings.

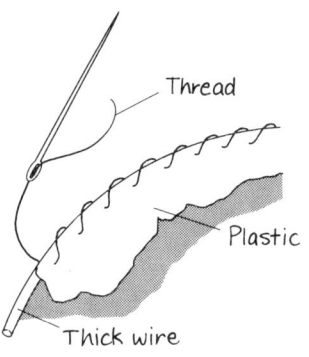

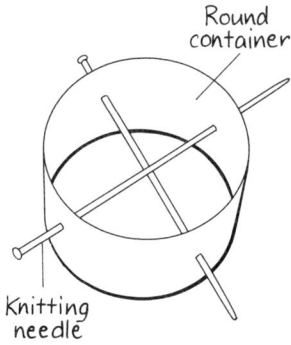

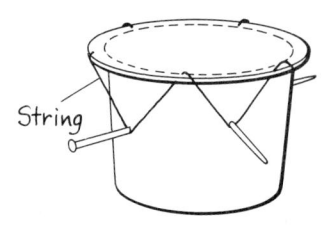

As you play, the plastic will stretch, so you will need to re-tie the strings fairly frequently at first. But the tension will soon settle down and you will be able to change the sound of your drum by squeezing together different sections of the string. As you squeeze, the note played by the drum head will get higher. When you release the tension, it will return to the original note. So you will be able to play at least two notes, one high and one low, and possibly several in between.

Use these different notes to copy the rhythm and shape of words. Or vice versa, make up a rhythm you like and find some words (they do not have to make sense) which fit the rhythm and will help you remember it. You should be able to memorize several different rhythms in this way.

Playing: A Drum Story

This piece is based on a dance-song composed and played by miners in Mozambique which criticises the white colonizers. Much African music deals with social issues and because by using drum language the music can literally 'talk', it is possible to say things which might be forbidden in ordinary speech. Here are the words to the song:

Line 1 Here they come, here they come,
Line 2 The English, the Dutch and the Portuguese.
Line 3 You put some of us in jail,
Line 4 But you will not finish all of us.
Line 5 Other young men are coming to join the dance.
Line 6 We will dance until we drop.

You are going to perform this song not by singing the words, but by 'talking' them on drums.

Preparation

Gather together as many different percussion instruments as possible, (drums, sticks, bells, etc.), and take one each. Hit your instrument a few times and get used to the sound it makes. Pick out three drums; the one which plays the lowest note, the one which plays the highest note, and one in between. These three drummers now play line 6 of the song, 'We will dance until we drop':

Repeat this until you know the rhythm well, then use the different sizes of drum to follow the natural rising and falling of the voice when speaking the words:

You will notice how the low and middle drums each play three times, but the high drum only once. What matters in this type of group playing is not how much you play, but that you play at the right time.

All the other players now join in; low sounds playing 'We will' and 'drop', middle-pitched sounds 'until we', and the high ones 'dance'. Repeat the line several times to establish the basic sound.

Some of you might like to add to the sound: you could lead up to your words with a few light taps, or a short drum roll. The main words in the sentence are 'dance' and 'drop' and these could be played more loudly. You can also add quicker, quieter notes between the main beats. In this way, you can create a complicated sound which is always interesting and changing. Everybody contributes, but nobody has to do anything particularly clever.

Now split into five groups. Each group takes a line of the song. Using the same methods as for line 6, work out how to play your line using the rhythm of the words and the different sounds of your instruments.

To play

Group 1 plays their line 'Here they come, here they come'. As they repeat it, members of the other groups join in until everyone is playing. When the line has been played several times and the sound has become full, the high drummer in group 1 signals the end of the line by hitting the high drum repeatedly and very loud. Everyone stops on the last word 'come'.

Then group 2 starts to play their line and the other instruments gradually join in. Each group plays their line in this way until you come to line 6, which is played by everybody from the beginning.

Play right through the piece more than once, trying to make the gaps between the lines shorter and the speed of picking up the rhythm of the words quicker. Also make the performance more expressive by playing louder for some lines than for others or getting louder or softer as you play a line.

DUDA

Bagpipe from Hungary

In Britain, the bagpipe is usually associated with marching and armies, but in most other countries, it is not used in this way. In Hungary the duda is thought of as a shepherd's instrument and often has the carved head of a ram or goat fitted to the top of the pipe.

They are playing the bagpipe
Down there, beyond the garden;
The shepherd boy is playing it,
In his heart's sorrow.

This Hungarian folk-song links the duda with shepherds and suggests that bagpipe music is used to express unhappiness. In fact, most music for the duda sounds quite happy to our ears; it is fast and is used to accompany energetic dancing. But folk musicians from all over the world believe that their music expresses the hardness of people's lives, and their deeper emotions such as love and sorrow. The next song gives a slightly different picture of the Hungarian bagpiper:

He who wants to become a piper, He must descend to hell;
There are living those pretty big dogs
The pretty big bagpipes are made from.

In Hungary, there are stories of the devil playing the duda, and this is another explanation for the carved goat's head as the goat has always been the devil's animal. The 'pretty big dogs the . . . bagpipes are made from' refers to the practice of using a whole animal skin for the bag which holds the air for playing the duda.

The Hungarian composer Béla Bartók collected this folk song:

Notice how this tune is put together using very few musical ideas: the first two bars consist of only three different notes which are then repeated to give bars 3 and 4. The melody shape of the first four bars is repeated exactly for bars 7 to 10 but begins on a lower note. The only snatch of tune which is not the same as the first two bars comes in bars 5 and 6. This 'motif' is repeated exactly, but using different notes, for the last two bars. So the whole tune is made up of only two tiny ideas.

This tune used to be very popular with duda players. Of course, a piper would change the tune in several ways: firstly, he would add a continuous low note known as a drone. Next, he would add a second drone which would alternate between two higher notes. Finally, he would alter the tune by leaving out some of the high notes because the chanter, (the pipe which plays the tune), does not have enough notes even for an economical melody such as this.

Things to do

1. Make a list of instruments which are associated with particular animals. Here are a couple: snake charmer's pipe, hunting horn.
2. Write a poem about someone who plays an instrument. If you sing a tune in your head as you are making up the words, it may help to give your poem a good rhythm.

Songs such as *Mr. Tambourine Man*, the nursery rhyme *Little Boy Blue* and the Christmas carol *The Little Drummer Boy* may give you a few ideas for poems about musicians.

Bagpipes throughout the world

This map misses out America, the Far East, Australia and most of Africa because the bagpipe is not native to any of these areas.

The Scottish Highland pipes have emigrated to every corner of the globe. They are best known for their use in marching bands but they also play a dignified solo music called pibroch.

The Irish uillean pipes are capable of playing very complicated music because as well as the drone, they are fitted with regulators which can sound chords to accompany the tune or play a second melody. No other bagpipe can do this. The bag is blown up by means of a bellows strapped to the player's elbow.

Bagpipes were popular in Northern Europe in medieval times. Pictures of feasts and fairs by artists such as Brueghel and Dürer nearly always have a fat, red-faced bagpiper in them.

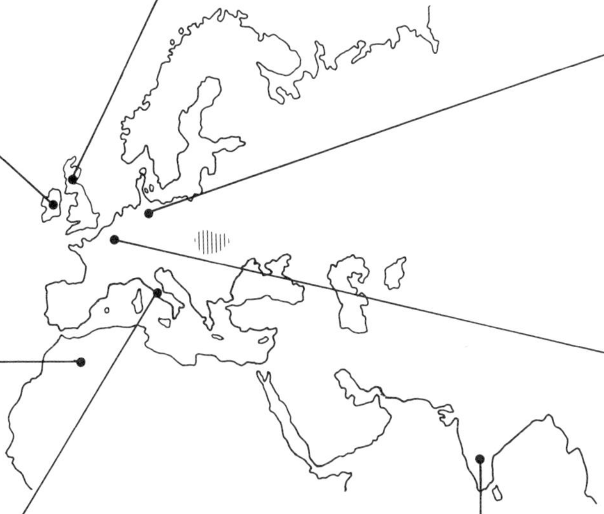

Bagpipes from North Africa are often known as hornpipes because the double chanters have animal horns fitted to the ends. They almost look like the animals from which they are made, and when they are filled with air and played, it is as if they were coming to life.

The musette was fashionable at the French court in the 18th century. It was usually highly ornate with ivory keys and a bag covered in silks and velvet. A far cry from the pig's bladder or goat skin still used in many countries.

The Italian zampogna is now found mainly in Sicily. It is often played in duet with the piffaro which is a sort of folk oboe.

Bagpipes in India are mainly used as drone instruments to accompany other players. Even though they may have a chanter as well as a drone pipe, both are never played together.

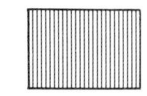

= area covered by the duda

Beethoven

Bartók (by the phonograph) collecting folksongs in a Hungarian village

Listening

Ludwig van Beethoven (1770–1827) was a German composer who spent most of his life in Vienna. At that time Vienna was the capital city of the Austro-Hungarian Empire so Beethoven would have had plenty of opportunities to hear Hungarian folk music, including the sound of the duda, in nearby villages. When he wrote his 'Pastoral' Symphony (No. 6 in F major), he wanted to express the 'awakening of happy feelings on getting into the country'. He did it like this:

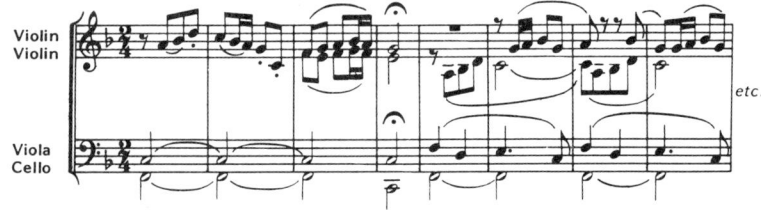

Using the string section of the orchestra, Beethoven gives us the unmistakable sound of the bagpipes; the lower instruments provide the drone while the violins play a snatch of a tune above. In between, the second violins put in some notes which start off as a melody but then become a temporary drone.

Listen to the whole of this movement. You will hear how the little motif which the violins play in bar 6 is repeated over and over by different instruments, and using different notes, in much the same way as the folk-song on page 20 is put together. Beethoven has used not only the sound of the duda, but the same method of composition.

Béla Bartók (1881–1945) wrote music which does not set out to 'awaken happy feelings' like Beethoven's 'Pastoral' Symphony. He wanted the music he studied among the Hungarian peasants to become part of his work as a composer. Most of his compositions show the influence of Hungarian folk music and many use the music of the duda. For instance, listen to *Swineherd's Dance* from the *Hungarian Sketches for Orchestra*, or piano works like *Sonatina*.

But it is in his large-scale works that the folk music influence is used to greatest effect. The second movement of Bartók's *Music for Strings, Percussion and Celeste* opens with these three motifs:

As the piece continues, the motifs are thrown about between the instruments, turned upside down, made even shorter and altered in many other ways. The overall effect is of vigorous, almost angry physical activity. Later on in the movement, Bartók uses some of the unusual rhythms common in Hungarian folk-dancing. If he is trying to give the listener an image of peasant life, it is closer to the 'heart's sorrow' of the bagpiper than to Beethoven's tourist brochure picture.

In the third movement of this piece, Bartók uses a drone, but by adding a kettledrum to the low strings and a fragmented, haunting tune above it, he succeeds in creating a sinister bagpiper, again not at all like Beethoven's.

Bartók is usually thought of as a nationalist composer who tried to write Hungarian music at a time when Hungary had just gained its independence from Austria, but his ambitions were much wider: 'My real idea . . . is the brotherhood of nations . . . I try to serve this idea in my music . . . and that is why I do not shut myself off from any influence'. By using folk music to write such powerful compositions, he became one of the most important composers of his time.

The continuing influence of the duda

The music of Bartók and his followers is deeply influenced by the duda. So are the pieces played by Hungarian gypsy bands.

Hungarian gypsy band

Towards the end of the 19th century, the job of playing at village weddings was taken over by gypsy bands. Gypsies have always adapted their music to what the audience expects to hear, so they copied the music of the duda. One of the main reasons for using gypsy bands rather than a bagpiper was the social prestige attached to being able to afford a lot of musicians.

Duda music could be adapted to group playing quite easily because it already had several distinct sounds in it: the drone bass was played by the double bass or cello, the violins played the tune whilst the second, alternating drone became a middle part using just a few notes. Even today, Hungarian gypsy bands still play in this style.

Apràja

Another peculiarity of Hungarian gypsy music which has been inherited from the duda is a way of ending a piece by squeezing together the notes of the melody to form very short motifs which are repeated lots of times. This process is called apràja.

At first, the motifs may be related to the tune just played, but then other motifs are introduced which can be used for any tune. It is rather like signing off a letter with some conventional phrase such as 'Yours sincerely'. The apràja section of a piece can be longer than the tune itself. It is a very useful way of ending dance music because it can easily lengthen the dance if the performers want to continue and can just as easily be cut off if they want to stop.

Playing exercise

First of all, learn to sing or play (on any instrument) the tune on page 20. As there are only two motifs in it, this should not take long.

Treat each two-bar phrase as an apràja motif. Sing them over and over one at a time. Now combine them. Bars 1 and 2 sung with 7 and 8 gives a severe sound, but with 5 and 6 the sound is more conventional.

When you have tried out the various combinations, perform the tune. Not from beginning to end but as a series of repeated motifs. Each performer chooses which two bars to sing, how many times to sing them and when to change. By chance, different motifs will combine and so the character of the piece will keep changing. Listen to this as you sing. Remain silent for a few bars if you wish. It does not matter which motif you sing, but it is essential that you keep to the same rhythm as everyone else.

Making a duda chanter

YOU WILL NEED

Plastic or wooden tubes closed off at one end (pen tops, empty pen casings, short lengths of bamboo or elderberry). Have a few spares in case of accidents.
A recorder or length of plastic piping 1–2 cm diameter
Sharp knife
Blu-tack or plasticine

HOW TO MAKE   **Time needed 10 minutes**

Make a reed in a tube by cutting into it with a sharp knife. You will need to scrape away a flat area first, then cut out three sides of a rectangle, leaving the reed attached by one short side.

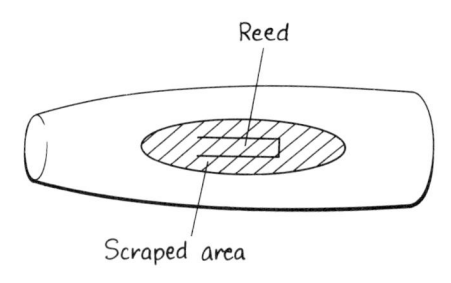

Bend back the free end of the reed a little, put the closed end of the tube into your mouth so that your lips are over the reed and blow. If the sound does not come straight away, scrape the reed a little thinner and make sure it is bent back just far enough for your breath to rush past and set it vibrating. You may need to make several until you get one with a really good, steady tone.

Fit your reed tube into the end of a recorder with the mouthpiece removed, using Blu-tack to make an airtight fit.

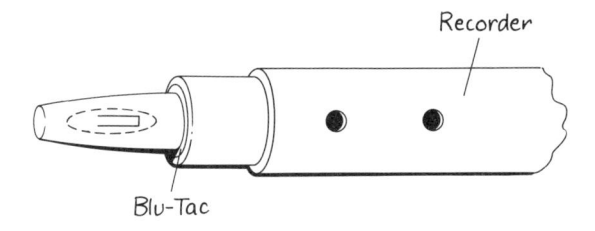

If you wish to make your own chanter rather than use a ready-made recorder, fit your tube into a length of plastic piping and cut finger-holes which suit the size of your hands.

Playing your duda chanter

It is now possible to play your chanter by putting the reed completely inside your mouth and blowing very hard. Move your fingers on the finger-holes as though you were playing a recorder or any other woodwind instrument.

If you have made your own chanter, now is the time to alter the notes it plays by plugging up finger-holes and cutting new ones if you are not satisfied with the sound.

By moving your fingers in regular patterns, you should be able to produce motifs which sound like those used on the duda, but your music will not really sound like a bagpipe because there are no drones to support the melody.

You can get around this problem by forming groups of three people. Two of you play a long, steady note, taking it in turns to breathe so that the sound is continuous. The third player adds a melody. It is not necessary for the drones to be in tune with the chanter pipe. In bagpipe music the main value of the drone is to provide the right background sound and the pitch is often rather unimportant.

Playing: Drones

The environment is full of drones; the buzzing of insects on a summer's day, the hum of distant traffic or electrical appliances, chatter behind a closed door, the wind in trees, the sound of running water, quiet music in shops and from transistor radios. These sounds form a continuous background against which other sounds stand out. We generally take notice of a sound when it is important, as when somebody speaks to us or a car sounds its horn. We rarely sit and listen to the background droning for its own sake.

This piece is a journey through some of the everyday drones we do not really listen to. Out of these come snatches of melody which build up into a sort of melody. Then the drones take over again and fade away.

Preparation
Split into five groups.

GROUP 1   **Animal drones**
Humming through paper on combs. Running finger along the top of a comb. Mouth noises (buzzing and squeaking). Bird-song.

GROUP 2   **Elemental drones**
Tapping on glass or wood. Blowing through pipes and into bottles. Pouring water. Flutes and recorders.

GROUP 3   **Human drones**
Voices talking quietly into tin cans, wastepaper baskets, etc. Chanting. Singing to yourself.

GROUP 4   **Musical drones**
Mouth organs, melodicas, dudas, pen-top drones, oboes, bassoons.

GROUP 5   **Mechanical drones**
Fans, flourescent lights. Voice imitations of engines in the distance. Electric organ, synthesizer. Radios and televisions.

Each group practises its own drone sound. Keep the sound quiet. One or two members of each group sing or play motifs from the tune on page 20. Make sure these motifs stand out from the background sound but do not play continuously, just scatter them about above the drone.

To play
You need a conductor. The conductor draws a large version of this spiral:

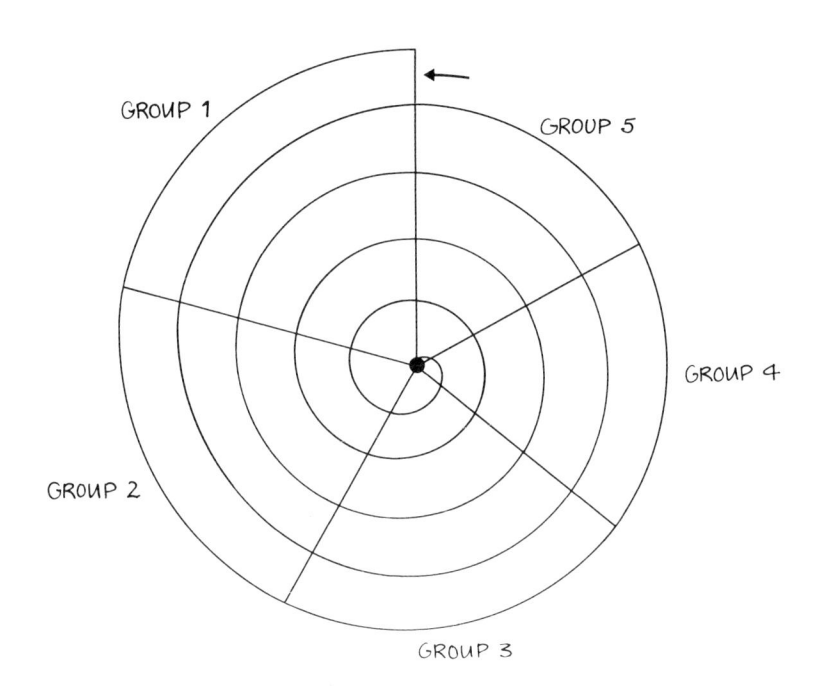

The sections can be coloured in. The piece starts when the conductor begins to move a finger around the spiral in an anti-clockwise direction. Group 1 starts to play and when the conductor moves into the next section, group 2 plays. There will be some overlapping of sound just as when you walk from one room into another and you can still hear the sounds from the first room. Do not worry about this overlapping and do not rush to finish the sound you are making. Fade out rather than stopping abruptly.

As the conductor goes further into the spiral, the drones will change more quickly until they are all playing at the same time in the centre circle. Here, the motifs which various members of each group are playing will combine in the same way as for the playing excercise on page 24.

The conductor waits in the centre circle for about 30 seconds, and then begins the journey back to the outside of the spiral. The drones become gradually more spaced out and eventually disappear.

DIDJERIDU
Trumpet from Australia

Aborigine rock painting

As you can see, a didjeridu looks nothing like a trumpet, but it belongs to the same family of instruments as a trumpet because of the way it is played. The player vibrates his lips while blowing into a long tube. This sets the column of air inside the tube vibrating as well and amplifies the sound.

To the Aborigines of Northern Australia, this sound is very important. The didjeridu is the only instrument they possess which is capable of producing a sustained note and it is essential to the success of the rituals where it is played.

Rituals are central to the Aborigines' way of life: they believe that life is a series of stages from childhood to old age and that it is necessary to be re-born when passing from one stage to the next. Rituals ensure that the passage between the different stages of life goes smoothly. Rituals also promote a harmonious social life and the continuation of natural species on which the Aborigines depend for food.

Music is also expected to help in making rain, an important function in the dry territories where Aborigines live. In 1968 a rain-making ritual was watched by an ethnomusicologist (person who studies the use of music in different cultures). The ritual consisted of recolouring a rock painting to the accompaniment of singing and dancing. When a light shower of rain followed the performance, the ethnomusicologist was surprised; it was the first for some time. But the Aborigines thought it was perfectly natural and to be expected. It was nothing to do with magic, just that they had performed the ritual properly.

Things to do

1. Take any tube (Smartie tube, short length of hose pipe, etc.) and blow into it, vibrating the lips. This is often referred to as 'blowing a raspberry' and results in a musical note coming out of the other end. This is the basic technique for playing all trumpets.

2. Make a drawing in the style of Aborigine rock paintings. There is one on this page and you will be able to find others in encyclopaedias and art books. Depict people dancing and musicians with instruments. Do not limit yourself to didjeridu players, draw people and instruments which are more familiar to you.

Trumpets throughout the world

It is often difficult to decide when an instrument is a trumpet and when it can better be described as a horn. Both types of instrument are played in the same way and have similar functions. This map includes horns and trumpets.

Brass bands consist of lip-vibrated instruments of various types and sizes. Western trumpets, horns and trombones are the most sophisticated development of all lip-vibrated instruments because they have valves or slides which enable them to play extra notes. Most trumpets from other cultures can only play one or two notes.

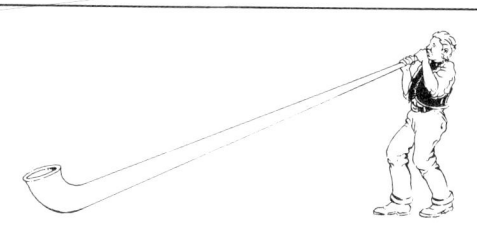

The Swiss alphorn is a very old wooden instrument used for sending signals over long distances. Although it is usually associated with the Alps, it is also found in other mountainous regions such as the Carpathians and the Pyrenees, and in Scandinavia.

African horns and trumpets are often spoken into rather than blown. This distorts the voice and, it is believed, makes it more likely to be heard by the gods. This instrument is carved from an elephant's tusk.

This Tibetan trumpet is made from a human thigh bone covered in yak skin and fitted with a copper bell decorated with semi-precious stones. It has a ceremonial use in religious festivals.

The Aztecs of ancient Mexico used trumpets made of a conch shell with a hole cut in one end. They were highly prized cult instruments associated with the rain god.

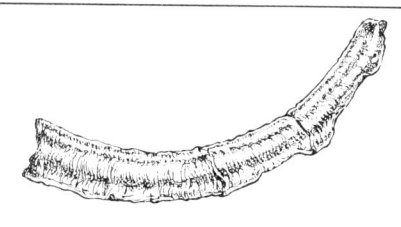

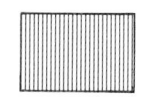

= area covered by the didjeridu

The shofar was played by the ancient Hebrews and has survived to the present day totally unchanged because of a religious law forbidding any alterations to it. It was the shofar (multiplied by the magic number seven) that was blown at Jericho 'when the walls came tumbling down'.

Making a didjeridu

Traditionally, a didjeridu was made from the branch of a tree which had been hollowed out by termites. It would often take longer to find a suitable branch than to make the instrument. Now it is more likely to be made from a length of plastic drainpipe.

YOU WILL NEED
1.5 metres of cardboard tubing (about 12 toilet roll innards or 3 of kitchen foil)
Sellotape

HOW TO MAKE   **Time needed 5 minutes**
Simply sellotape together the tubes to form one continuous tube. Decorate it if you wish.

How to play your didjeridu
You already know how to use lip vibration to produce a sound. Blow into the didjeridu and adjust the tension of your lips until you produce a pitch which sets the whole tube vibrating.

This is the basic tone of all didjeridu playing and is in general the only note used. However, skilful players modify this sound in several ways to produce a rich and complex music.

1. Continuous blowing. You need a lot of breath to make a didjeridu speak, so the notes tend to be short. Good players try to produce a continuous tone by breathing in at the same time as they are playing. To do this, use your cheeks as a pair of bellows, store air in them and then use the muscles to push the air out while you breathe in through the nose.
2. In addition to this fundamental tone, players often sing into the didjeridu. Singing a long, held note over the fundamental tone can result in full chords sounding. Other sung notes which clash with the fundamental tone make rhythmic beats.
3. The player may interrupt the basic tone with sudden explosive sounds or squeaks or grunts which imitate birds or animals.

Playing exercise
The didjeridu is nearly always accompanied by the beating of sticks. Because the sticks may play in several different rhythms at the same time, this can result in some exciting sounds.

Split into four groups.

GROUP 1   Claps
Clap at a regular speed without making any of the claps stand out by being louder than the others.

GROUP 2   Stamps
Stamp on every other clap.

GROUP 3   Grunts
Grunt on every third clap.

GROUP 4   Didjeridus
Play didjeridus half-way between every grunt.

In musical notation it looks like this:

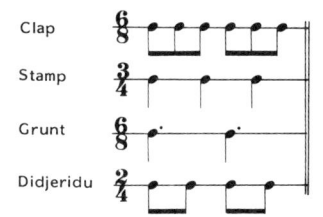

Learning to play in aboriginal society
Aboriginal women and children have their own rituals and do not often join in the secret rituals of the men. So there are not many opportunities for young boys to learn how to play the didjeridu. But children come together with adults for some non-secret rituals and so gradually absorb the dances and music. They will then copy the adult behaviour in their own play rituals.

Secret, sacred music is fast disappearing amongst the Aborigines, but non-secret music is on the increase and the playing of the didjeridu is spreading from the north to other areas of Australia. In the north, most men play the didjeridu, but a virtuoso is rare and a good player can expect to earn some money for his skill.

Young man playing the didjeridu

Playing: Picture-drawing Music

The didjeridu is very rarely played solo. It is usually part of a bigger activity involving singing, dancing, prayer, teaching, playing other instruments and often painting or drawing pictures. The popular Australian entertainer Rolf Harris paints pictures to music during his television shows. Maybe he got the idea from the Aborigines.

Preparation

Three people are appointed artists and the rest are musicians. The musicians split into three groups identified by a colour, and practise their own sounds.

GROUP 1   Yellow
This group's music represents the dancers. Play sticks, rasps, wood blocks, hand-clapping and didjeridus in the playing exercise given on page 28. If you would rather make up your own rhythms, then do so. Remember to build up the sound slowly, start with one player keeping a regular beat, then gradually add other beats to it, always making sure the distance between each of your beats is the same. Once there are three or four people playing, do not think that you have to take your beat from the first player. Use any beat you like and divide it evenly or multiply it.

GROUP 2   Red
This music represents the Australian desert. Play didjeridus, the strings of a piano, cymbals and gongs. The didjeridus play long, steady, low notes. If you cannot manage continuous blowing, then get together in pairs and take it in turns to breathe. Against this continuous background play very high notes on the piano by brushing a finger against the top strings, and make occasional shimmering noises on suspended cymbals and gongs.

GROUP 3   Blue
'The dreaming' was a time when the earth was without form. 'Powers' moved about the earth and created mountains, seas, plants, animals and human society. Aborigines think that all creativity comes from this time, so when they want a new song or dance, they 'follow up the dreaming'. They do this by going into a trance.

This group plays trance-like music on didjeridus, lengths of piping, horns, trombones and other low brass instruments to make a deep, throbbing sound. Play the lowest note you can find for a very long time, but interrupt the sound at regular intervals by putting your tongue between your lips. Everyone plays their own note at their own speed to produce a really heavy sound.

The artists
While the groups are practising their music, the artists choose one of the rock drawings made during the 'Things to do' on page 26. They prepare a huge version of it on a blackboard with white chalk.

To play

Each artist takes a different coloured chalk: yellow, red, blue. Taking turns and occasionally working two at a time, or even all together, they colour in the drawing. The groups play when their colour is being used on the drawing and stop when their artist takes a rest.

So the artists are telling the musicians what to do through their drawing. This means that they must not become too involved in the colouring but keep an ear for what is happening in the music. When the picture is completed, all three groups play together until instructed to stop by the artists putting down their chalk.

Ayers rock, a sandstone outcrop in the Australian desert

SITAR

Lute from North India

Sitar players (second left and second right) in an Indian band

'Sitar' sounds a bit like 'guitar' and the two instruments are in fact related. They belong to a family of instruments known as lutes which have strings stretched over a neck and some sort of box or bowl at the end to amplify the sound. Organologists (people who study instruments and their history) believe that lutes were first invented in Persia and spread eastward into India and the Far East and westward into North Africa and Europe.

The 'setar' is a modern Persian instrument. The name means 'five strings' but its Indian namesake the sitar may have up to twenty strings! Which just goes to show how misleading names can sometimes be. But sitarists use only two or three strings to play melodies, the rest are divided between drone strings and sympathetic strings. It is these extra strings which give the sitar its characteristic sound; the sympathetic strings are not plucked by the player but pick up vibrations from the melody strings to make a faint, twangy echo.

The following tune is played by sitarists as part of an exercise to practise Rag Yaman Kalyan ('Rag' is pronounced with a long 'a' as in 'party').

But Rag Yaman Kalyan would never sound like this in performance. The reason for this is that all serious players of North Indian music use improvisation, that is, they do not perform set pieces, but make up the notes as they go along.

Improvisation could be chaotic if the performers did not follow very definite guidelines which make sure the piece they are playing is Rag Yaman Kalyan and not Rag something else. It is a bit like giving a talk on a subject which interests you; you make up the words and sentences as you go along, but you have a clear idea of what you are going to say because you have set certain limits on yourself. The other thing which limits your speech is the grammar of your language; if you did not speak according to certain rules (even though you may not understand them fully, you still use them), no one else would understand you.

So when an Indian musician improvises on a rag he is not playing whichever notes he fancies, he is playing only the notes which occur in that Rag and within the limits of the 'grammar' of Indian music.

Things to do

1. Here is an experiment to hear how a sympathetic string works: play a note in the middle of the piano, then lift your finger off the key and notice how the sound stops. Now with the left hand press down a fistful of notes at the bottom of the keyboard. Wait for any notes you played to die away completely. Now play the original note again, still holding down the keys with the left hand. This time when you release the key, the sound will continue and you may be able to hear a few extra notes as well.

Look inside the piano and repeat the experiment. Work out why this happens and write a few lines explaining it.

2. Have an improvised conversation. Sit in a circle and speak one at a time. Here are the rules:

a) Never stray from the subject.
b) Silences must last for no more than five seconds.
c) Each speaker must use at least two words which the previous speaker also used.
d) However, you must not copy previous speakers word for word.
e) You must make sense.
f) Your conversation must be grammatical.

Lutes throughout the world

The banjo was introduced into the United States by West African slaves in the 18th century. It was adopted by the white settlers and eventually exported to Europe.

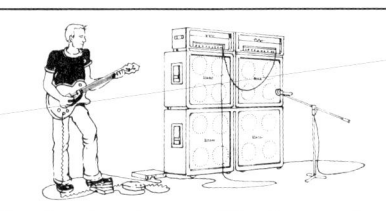

The electric guitar amplifies its sound electronically, so it does not actually need a soundbox. But most instruments still have bodies which look like soundboxes, though they may be very unusual shapes.

The Russian balalaika is a three-stringed lute with a triangular body. Nowadays it is made in six sizes and can be played in large bands to give a full orchestral effect.

The samisen from Japan is played with a huge and odd-shaped plectrum made of bone. After playing the string, this plectrum slaps against the belly of the samisen to give a percussive as well as a plucked sound.

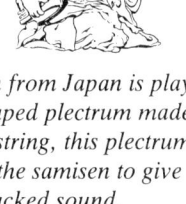

The West African kora is a cross between a harp and a lute. Up to twenty strings are stretched over a bridge in the same way as a lute, but each string only plays one note as in the harp.

The 'ūd is an Arabic instrument which was the direct ancestor of the European lute. It does not have any frets, so the player has to find the correct place for his fingers by the sound of the string.

The tanbur or tambura is found in most countries from the Balkans to India. It is different in every country and sometimes in every area of a country. In general it has a long neck with frets and a small, pear-shaped body.

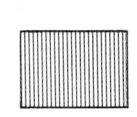

▦ = area covered by the sitar

31

Listening

Nowadays, everyone knows the sound of the sitar. It was popularized in the West by groups such as the Beatles in the 1960s. This led to an interest in the original music of the sitar and to performances by famous Indian musicians like Ravi Shankar, whose concerts were often attended by thousands of enthusiastic young people.

Indian music has now lost some of its mass appeal, but it is still possible to hear live concerts as there is enough interest for performers to visit Europe from India on a regular basis. You can also hear Indian music on the Asian language television and radio programmes. A lot of these broadcasts consist of film music which is closer to our pop music than to the sort of music usually played on the sitar, but you will also hear some more traditional Indian music.

Modern pop groups such as Blancmange and Monsoon are still using the sitar in their compositions. Art music composers have written some music for sitar but it has not become a regular part of Western ensembles.

Ravi Shankar with George Harrison of The Beatles

Here is a song written by George Harrison and performed by the Beatles on their famous album *Sergeant Pepper's Lonely Hearts Club Band*. The tune is played on the sitar:

Within You Without You

The tune suits the sound of the sitar and has other Indian features: the melody does not end in a conventional 'final' way as we expect Western melodies to do, and the accompaniment on the original recording was not a series of chords on the guitar, but simple drones.

But the influence of India on George Harrison went further than just copying the sounds of Indian music. Here are the words to *Within You Without You*:

We were talking about the space between us all,
And the people who hide themselves behind a wall of illusion,
Never glimpse the truth,
Then it's far too late when they pass away.

We were talking about the love we all could share,
When we find it to try our best to hold it there with our love,
With our love we could save the world.

We were talking about the love that's gone so cold,
And the people who gain the world and lose their soul,
They don't know, they can't see,
Are you one of them?

Try to realize it's all within yourself,
No one else can make you change.
And to see you're really only very small
And life flows on within you and without you.

As well as learning to play the sitar, George Harrison took up meditation and other aspects of Indian culture. This song talks of some of the things that he thought were wrong about a Western lifestyle and how to change them. His conclusions come from Indian philosophy: do not lie to yourself, love everyone, material wealth is less important than your soul, individuals are unimportant, do not live in a world of your own but become part of the universe. So the use of Indian sounds in this song is appropriate to its mood and meaning.

Learning to play the sitar

The traditional way of learning to play an instrument in India is for the pupil to go and live in the home of his guru (teacher) and to spend many years getting to know and understand the various rags. Because the player will eventually perform his own version of each rag, it is essential that he knows the rules thoroughly and this requires long and painstaking preparation.

In modern India, it is not so easy to find a guru who will take on pupils in this way, and there is now a lot of demand for music lessons, especially from girls who want to improve their chances of finding a husband. So most music students nowadays learn at music colleges or by visiting the home of a teacher on a regular basis.

Although the old relationship between pupil and guru is disappearing, it is still necessary for the trainee musician to receive several hours of instruction every week. This is done by attending lessons not once a week as we usually do in this country, but by having a lesson every day, often very early in the morning.

A typical sitar class

Sargam

Lessons mainly consist of repeating exercises given by the teacher, listening to him and playing along with him. Music is never played from notation.

But Indian music does have a method of writing down music called sargam notation. It works in much the same way as the Western solfa system of singing; there are seven syllables for the seven notes of the Indian scale. The eighth note with the dot above it is one octave above the first note:

sa   re   ga   ma   pa   dha   ni   sȧ

These correspond exactly to our major scale:

do   re   mi   fa   so   la   ti   do

Because Indian music is passed on from teacher to pupil by ear, these syllables are more likely to be spoken or sung than written down. It is quite common to hear singers using these syllables instead of words, even during performance.

Playing exercise

Sing a scale using the sargam syllables rather than do–re–mi. Do it a few times going up and back down. Take a well-known song and substitute sargam syllables for the words. For instance, do you recognize this tune?

ga   re   sa   ga   re   sa
pa   ma ma   ga   pa   ma ma   ga

Once you have got the hang of this, try singing the tune on page 30 using sargam. It begins:

ga   re   ga   ṇi   sa   re

The dot underneath 'ni' shows that it sounds in the octave below 'sa', not above it.

You could also sing the tune for *Within You Without You* using sargam. In this tune, 'ni' would need to be sung flat (a little lower). This is shown by a line beneath the note, so the tune would start:

ga   ma   pa   ni̱

Making a tambura

The sitar is too complicated to try and copy, but the tambura looks similar and does not need frets or sympathetic strings. It is an essential part of any Indian ensemble, vocal or instrumental, because it provides the drone sound which is the characteristic background to all Indian music.

YOU WILL NEED
A length of dowelling or broom handle (about 1 m)
4 pieces of wire 50 cm longer than the dowelling (fuse wire, telephone wire, old strings from a piano, guitar or banjo)
4 beads with holes all the way through
A long nail
A screw hook
A plastic bowl (a margarine tub is ideal)
Piece of thick cardboard
Piece of pencil (hexagonal)
Sellotape
Sharp knife
Hammer

HOW TO MAKE   **Time needed 20 minutes**

Hammer the nail through one end of the dowel rod so that the same amount sticks out on each side. Make holes in the plastic bowl near to the rim and push the other end of the dowel rod through. About 5 cm should protrude from the bowl at the bottom. Screw the hook into this and fix the dowel rod to he bowl with sellotape, as shown on the left.

Now cut a circle of cardboard the same size as the rim of the bowl and fix this to the front of your instrument. Wind one end of a piece of wire back onto itself to make a small loop. Do not make this winding too long (it should be shorter than the distance from the screw hook to the bowl). Thread a bead onto the wire from the other end.

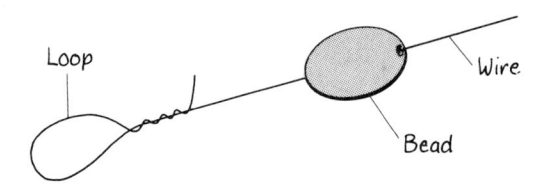

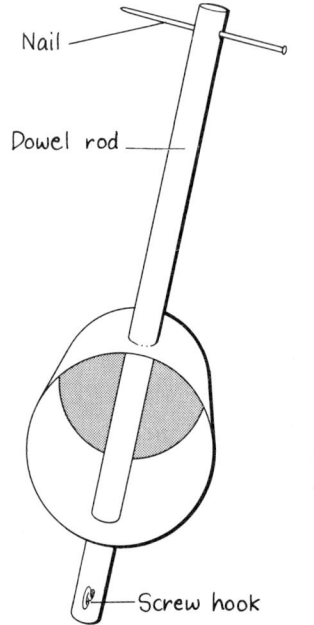

Next, put the loop over the screw hook and stretch the wire to the other end of the dowel rod. Pulling tightly, wrap the wire several times around the nail and finish with a knot. Repeat this for each of the other three strings, fixing two to each half of the nail.

Slide the piece of pencil between the strings and the cardboard circle. It should be held fairly securely by the tension of the strings. Cut four grooves at even spaces along the top side of the pencil and slide the strings into them.

Your instrument is now finished and should look something like this:

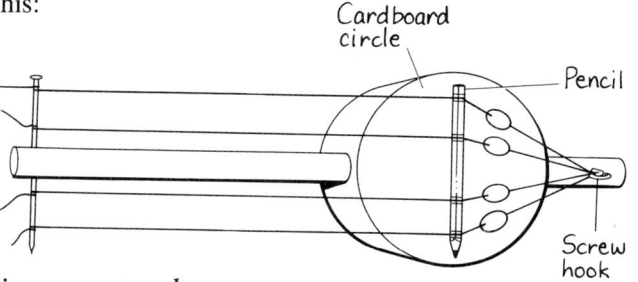

Playing your tambura
Sit on the floor. Hold your instrument vertically and rest the neck on your left shoulder. Using the fingers of your left hand, pluck the strings one by one about two-thirds of the way up the strings. This should make a thin and slightly buzzy sound.

At this point, the tuning of the strings is completely accidental, depending on the tension of the wire, but the beads can be used to control the tuning. If you push one towards the screw hook, it should press against the cardboard and stretch the string a little more, making the note higher. If this does not work, place some folded paper under the bead to raise it.

Tambura strings are usually tuned to 'sa' and 'pa', with optional 'ni' or 'ga'. Try tuning the strings to these notes using the tuning beads. Pick one of the lower-sounding strings as 'sa' and sing up the scale to find 'pa'. If two or even three strings play the same note, it does not matter.

Now play the strings of your tambura in a regular rhythm. For instance:

1, 2, 3, 4, rest

Repeat over and over. This sound, with all the strings vibrating at once, forms the background to nearly all Indian classical music. The rhythm of plucking the tambura strings bears no relationship to the rhythm of the piece being played. This sound is used in the piece on the next page.

Playing: Tal

Tal is a way of dividing a rag into short sections all of the same length. Learn how to 'keep the tal' by counting on your fingers. As there is no conductor in Indian music, all members of the audience keep time for themselves like this.

Here is a tal with 16 beats divided into four groups of four beats each. Beats 2, 3, and 4 of each group are counted by tapping the thumb of the right hand against different fingers:

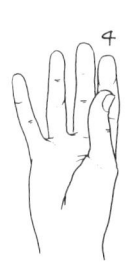

The first beat of each group is counted either by a silent clap or a wave of the right hand. The claps come on the first, second and last groups (marked X, 2 and 3) and the wave comes on the third (marked O). So the whole pattern looks like this:

X				2				0				3			
1	2	3	4	5	6	7	8	9	10	11	12	13	14	15	16
Clap	tap	tap	tap	Clap	tap	tap	tap	Wave	tap	tap	tap	Clap	tap	tap	tap

Practise this until you can do it without having to concentrate too hard. You will notice that the signs above each group of four beats are the same as those above the tune on page 30. Half of you beat out the tal while the other half sing the tune and see how the two fit together.

Preparation
Split into four groups.

GROUP 1   Timekeepers
This group does not play the music, but stands facing the musicians and beats out the tal to help them keep in time. At Indian concerts, some members of the audience do this. You will need to exaggerate your hand movements, especially the wave, so that the musicians can follow the tal easily. Draw a large version of the following diagram (colour in the segments) and place it behind you.

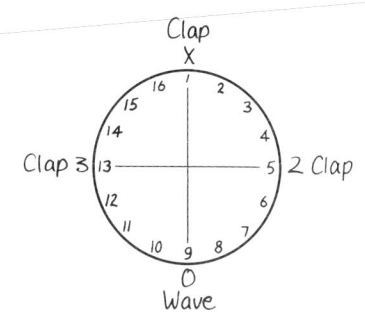

GROUP 2   Drummers
Take a drum and experiment tapping it with the fingers. The sound is quiet, but you can play very fast. You have the freedom to play whatever you want. You do not have to mark out the rhythm, the timekeepers are doing that, but you must try to play in such a way as to suggest the rhythm of the tal. This means taking notice of the 'empty' beat half way through the tal (where the timekeepers wave) and making the sound noticeably lighter at that point.

GROUP 3   Soloists
Singers and any instrumentalists. Your job is to play the tune from page 30 in time with the tal. Also, each person in this group makes up their own variation on the tune. It must last for exactly one cycle of the tal.

GROUP 4   Drones
Tamburas, violins, cellos, electric keyboards, etc. Tune your instruments to 'sa', 'ga', 'pa' and 'ni', (take 'sa' as the last note of the melody played by group 3). Practise playing your drones in a rhythm completely independent of the tal. Also sing through the tune a few times. Once the piece starts, you may like to join in with the soloists.

To play
The timekeepers beat through one whole cycle of the tal as group 4 gradually bring in their drones. At the beginning of the second cycle, the other two groups join in. Group 3 play the tune.

On the third cycle, one member of group 3 plays the variation he or she has worked out. Other members of group 3 remain silent and the other groups play more softly.

During the next cycle, all group 3 play the tune again and group 4 join in singing the tune. Then another member of group 3 takes a solo, and so on until all members of group 3 have played their variations. Then play through the tune twice and finish.

GENDER

Metal xylophone from Indonesia

Indonesia is a collection of some 3,000 islands between the mainland of South-east Asia and Australia. Percussion instruments which play a musical note rather than an unpitched sound have been used there for thousands of years and have spread to other cultures throughout the world.

The gender (pronounce 'g' as in 'gun' and the final 'er' as 'air') is one of the most important of these 'tuned percussion' instruments. In the Wajang Kulit (shadow puppet play) it is used to accompany the voice of the puppeteer and it is often played by his wife because whoever provides the music for these plays needs to know the stories in great detail.

Indonesian puppet theatre cannot be compared to our seaside Punch and Judy shows. It is a major form of art and entertainment, and one show may last for several hours. Puppeteers earn huge sums of money, even by Western standards, and the stories they tell, though based on traditional epics, include scenes of satire and social comment. This song deals with overpopulation, a serious problem for Indonesia.

Remember, please remember, friends who are living now,
So that we don't make difficulties for our descendants,
Society must be ordered and in harmony.
Also, the many children of our era, it is best, it is necessary, must be limited according to one's salary,
In order that stability be reached, each family must be thankful and feel content with two, at the very most three.

It is sung to the following tune:

The gender is also a leading member of Indonesian orchestras called gamelan. In these orchestras, which mainly consist of tuned percussion instruments, the gender has two important functions. Firstly it plays variations on the main melody and secondly, because both hands are used, it can play more than one melody at a time, which adds interest to the overall sound.

Things to do

1. The gender is a type of instrument known as an idiophone, which means that it produces a sound from the vibrations of its own body. Any solid object is a potential idiophone.

Experiment with a few objects you have around you. Metal cutlery, pieces of wood, pottery, etc. Hit them and listen to the sound they make. Is it bright or dull? Most sounds die away quickly. Can you make them last for longer?

2. Look at the instruments on the next page and read about them. Use this information to write a description of how xylophones reached South America from Indonesia.

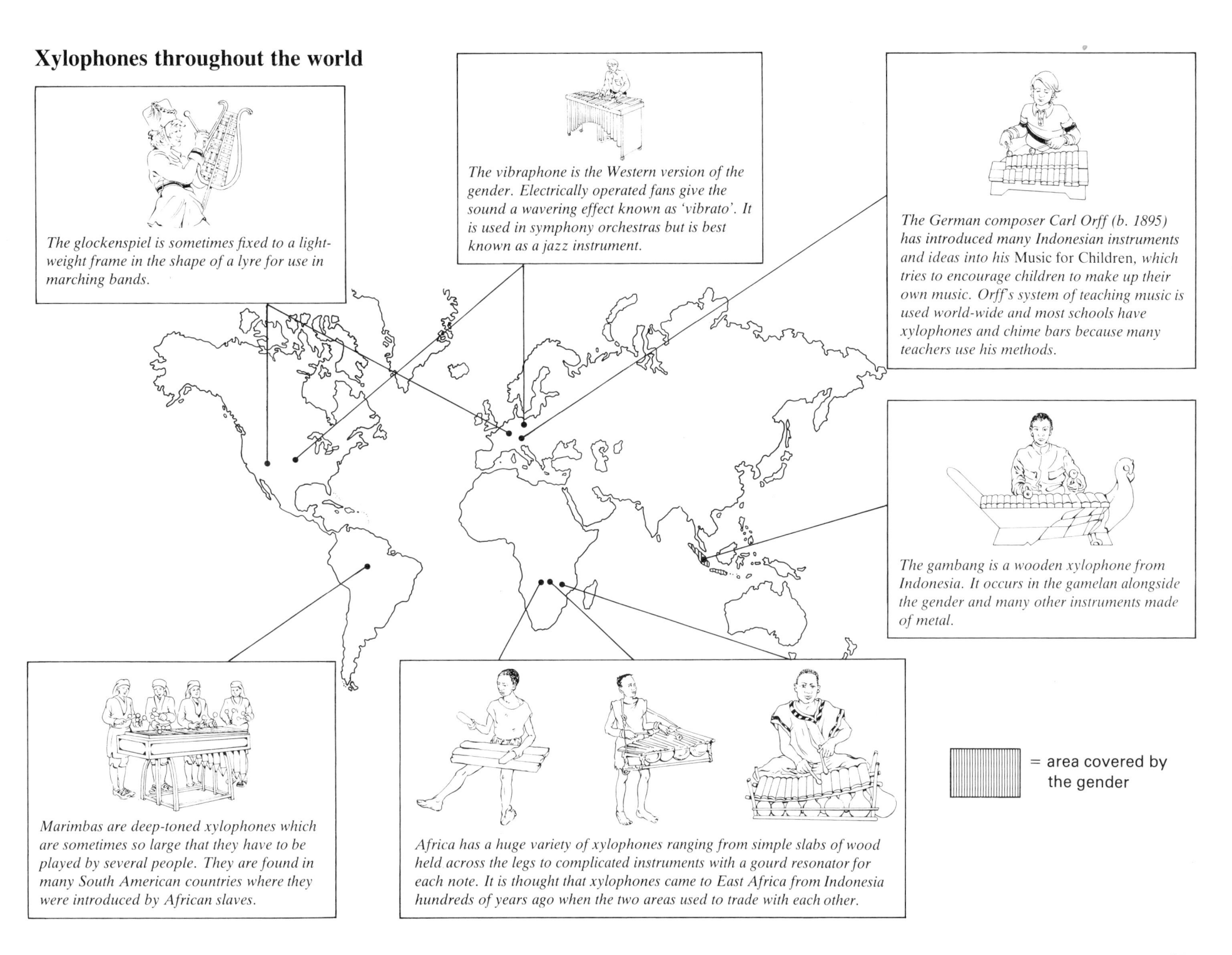

Xylophones throughout the world

The glockenspiel is sometimes fixed to a lightweight frame in the shape of a lyre for use in marching bands.

The vibraphone is the Western version of the gender. Electrically operated fans give the sound a wavering effect known as 'vibrato'. It is used in symphony orchestras but is best known as a jazz instrument.

The German composer Carl Orff (b. 1895) has introduced many Indonesian instruments and ideas into his Music for Children, *which tries to encourage children to make up their own music. Orff's system of teaching music is used world-wide and most schools have xylophones and chime bars because many teachers use his methods.*

The gambang is a wooden xylophone from Indonesia. It occurs in the gamelan alongside the gender and many other instruments made of metal.

Marimbas are deep-toned xylophones which are sometimes so large that they have to be played by several people. They are found in many South American countries where they were introduced by African slaves.

Africa has a huge variety of xylophones ranging from simple slabs of wood held across the legs to complicated instruments with a gourd resonator for each note. It is thought that xylophones came to East Africa from Indonesia hundreds of years ago when the two areas used to trade with each other.

= area covered by the gender

Claude Debussy

Listening

Before the invention of the gramophone, Europeans had very few opportunities to hear music from Oriental countries. But in 1889, groups of musicians from all over the world were brought to play at the Paris Exhibition. One group was a gamelan orchestra from Java and many composers were deeply impressed by the unusual sound. The French composer Claude Debussy (1862–1918) wrote to a friend:

> 'If we listen without prejudice to the charm of their percussion we must confess that our percussion is like primitive noises at a country fair'.

Debussy soon began using ideas from the gamelan in his compositions such as *Nuages* (from *Nocturnes for Orchestra*):

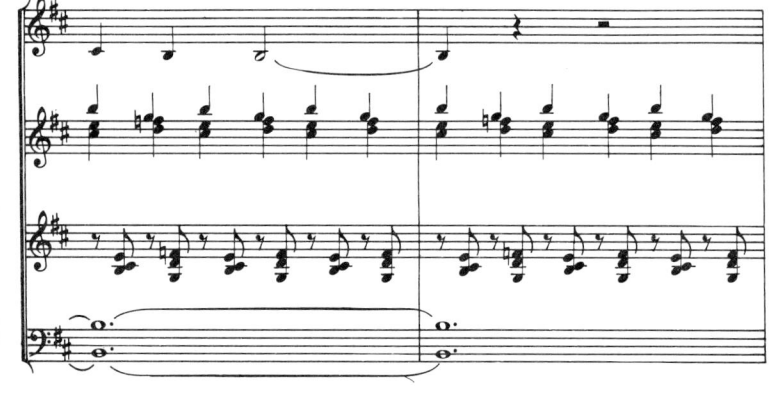

Record cover to Mike Oldfield's 'Tubular Bells'

Here, the string section of the orchestra is split up in the same way as a gamelan. The double bass plays a long, held note like a huge gong. Above, the violins rock between notes like the gender while the violas and cellos pluck their strings (pizzicato) after every violin note for a dry sound which imitates the wooden gambang. The cor anglais adds a snatch of melody known as a motif.

Debussy used this delicate sound in other pieces such as *La Mer*. Benjamin Britten (1913–1976) was an English composer who was also influenced by Indonesian music. Because he believed that people throughout the world should learn about and respect each other's cultures, he often used sounds he had heard in other countries in his own pieces.

His music for the ballet *The Prince of the Pagodas* uses gamelan music from the Indonesian island of Bali. This is very different from the Javanese music which inspired Debussy. It is much louder and more rhythmically exciting.

This sound, employing all the bright-toned percussion instruments of the modern orchestra is used by Britten whenever he wants to create an other-worldly atmosphere in his music. It can also be found in his *War Requiem* (the *Sanctus*), *Curlew River*, and in his last opera *Death in Venice* where it is associated with Tadzio, the young boy who is one of the main characters.

Indonesian music has given ideas to many other contemporary composers. Carl Orff in his educational work, and the modern American composer Steve Reich both show the influence of gamelan in the way music can be created and played by groups of people working together.

Much modern popular music such as Mike Oldfield's *Tubular Bells* would be unthinkable without ideas we have borrowed from Indonesian music.

Learning to play the gender

Traditionally, Indonesian children are never given music lessons. They learn their music by attending lots of gamelan rehearsals and performances and gradually picking up all they need to know.

When he is about five, the budding gender player might start playing the melody of a piece on the saron, a metal xylophone played with only one beater. He then progresses through all the instruments of the gamelan, finishing up with the gender when he becomes an adult.

Village musicians are still trained in this way, but in the cities, there are music schools and 'gamelan clubs' where boys and girls can go to learn in a more formal way. Although girls are now able to play in the gamelan, they do not mix with the boys, but form all-female ensembles.

At these schools, teaching is always in groups. To play in a gamelan successfully, it is not necessary to have a wonderful technique on your instrument, but it is essential that you understand how your part contributes to the overall sound and to keep time without a conductor. Group lessons are the best way to develop this understanding. However, gender players are sometimes given individual tuition because of the complexities involved in playing more than one melody at the same time.

Gamelan outside Indonesia

Indonesia used to be a Dutch colony, so it is hardly surprising that the first non-Indonesian gamelan was founded in the Netherlands in the 1950s. Since then, the playing of gamelan has spread throughout Europe and to America and Australia.

There are now several gamelans in Britain giving regular concerts, and groups from Indonesia also visit frequently. So it is possible to hear live gamelan music in this country. It is a wonderful experience. Because of the deep vibrations of the huge gongs, you seem to feel the music as well as hear it.

Playing exercises

Indonesian musicians refer to notes by number. The black notes of the piano roughly correspond to an Indonesian scale called slendro. By numbering these notes from 1 to 5 (it does not matter which note you start on) it is possible to play melodies which have the characteristic shape and sound of Indonesian music. Now play these notes and listen to the pattern:

2123 4543 2321 2343

If you want to write melodies that are higher or lower than these five notes, you can move up into the next group of black notes by putting a dot above the numbers, or down to the notes below by putting a dot underneath. It is now possible to write down melodies covering three octaves:

5 $\dot{1}$ $\dot{2}$ $\dot{3}$ $\dot{2}$ $\dot{1}$ 5 4 3 2 1 3 4 3 2 3 2 $\underset{.}{4}$ $\underset{.}{5}$ 1 3 4 $\underset{.}{5}$ $\underset{.}{2}$ $\underset{.}{3}$ *etc.*

Try making up your own melodies in this way and teaching them to other people by number notation.

For variety, change some of the notes. For instance change note 1 to a white note and hear how this affects the mood of your melody.

Gong section of the gamelan orchestra, played by a Western musician

Making a gender

YOU WILL NEED

5 solid metal knives (suspend them by a rubber band and hit them to make sure they play five different notes)
A breakfast cereal packet
2 pieces of wood the same length as the cereal packet
12 nails
Rubber bands
5 cardboard tubes (inside of toilet rolls or Smartie tubes)
Sellotape
Sand
Glue

HOW TO MAKE **Time needed 30 minutes**

Cut the cereal packet to the same size as your cardboard tubes. Glue the tubes to the inside of the packet, making sure they are fixed firmly at the bottom.

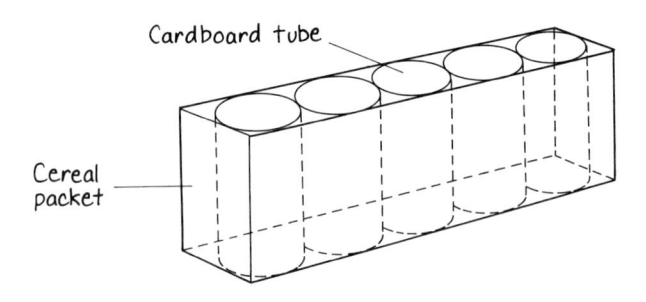

Hammer 6 nails into each piece of wood at regular intervals, leaving plenty of nail above the wood. Stick a piece of wood to each side of the cereal packet with the nails sticking up. Use glue and Sellotape for extra strength.

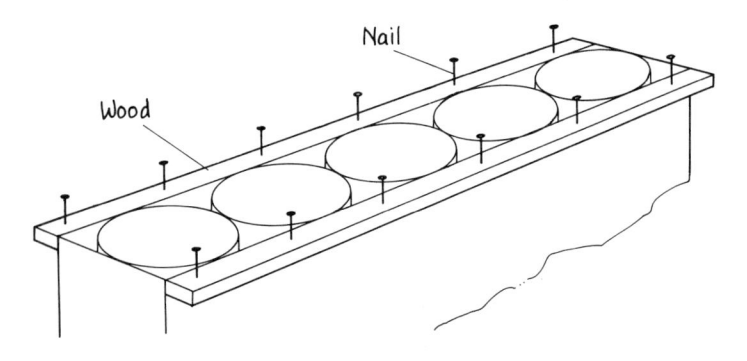

Now fix one knive horizontally above each resonator tube by stretching rubber bands between the nails and pushing the knife between them.

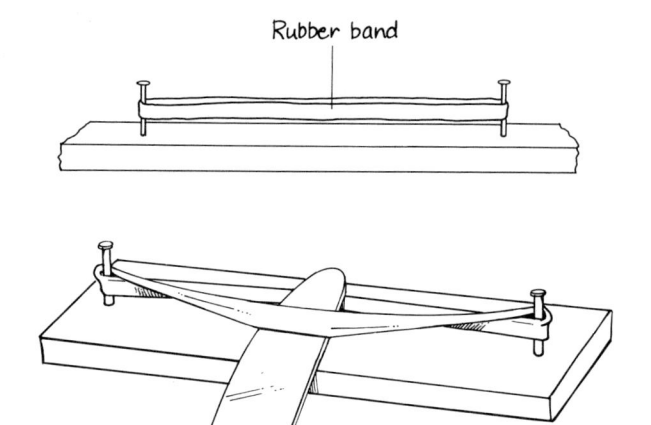

Each resonator tube should produce the same note as the knife hanging over it. To check this, blow across the top of the tube and you should be able to hear a faint, flute-like note. Fill the resonator with sand until this note is the same as that of its knife.

Playing your gender

Use a padded beater. Hit one of the knives. It should make a soft but vibrant sound which carries well because of the individually tuned resonator.

When you play the next knife, stop the first one vibrating by gently holding one end between the thumb and forefinger of your free hand. In this way, you will only hear one note at a time and the tune will stand out clearly.

Playing: Gending

This composition takes its name from the Indonesian word meaning 'a piece of music'. All gendings are formed by repeating an 'inner melody' several times with slight variations on some of the instruments. The music seems to go round and round like a big wheel.

Preparation

Choose an instrument and learn to recognize the symbol used for it in the score.

- H — High piano
- M — Middle piano
- L — Low piano
- ⊙ — Gong and suspended cymbal
- ▯ — Tubular bells
- ▯ — Glockenspiel
- ▯ — Gender
- L — Low xylophone
- H — High xylophone
- ▬ — Wood block

The short 'inner melody' is given in number notation in the circles joined by double lines. You play every time the symbol for your instrument is shown on one of the spokes of the wheel. The number notation on the outside of the wheel is a variation on the inner melody for those playing more notes in each cycle.

Practise the notes for your instrument, moving clockwise around the circle.

To play

In order to play all together, you need to move from spoke to spoke at an even pace. Treat the instruments on the inside of the circle as 'time-markers'. These instruments divide the wheel into eight equal parts. Listen to them playing and you will hear this as eight beats. If your instrument plays on the spokes which come 16 times, you simply play the extra notes half way between the existing beats, If you are playing on the outside of the wheel where the notes occur 32 times per cycle, you have to divide the beat yet again.

Start at the arrow and go round the circle as many times as you like, ending on the full stop.

Further developments

Try making up your own melody by changing the notes inside the hub of the wheel. This will sound like a completely different piece even though you will be reading from the same score.

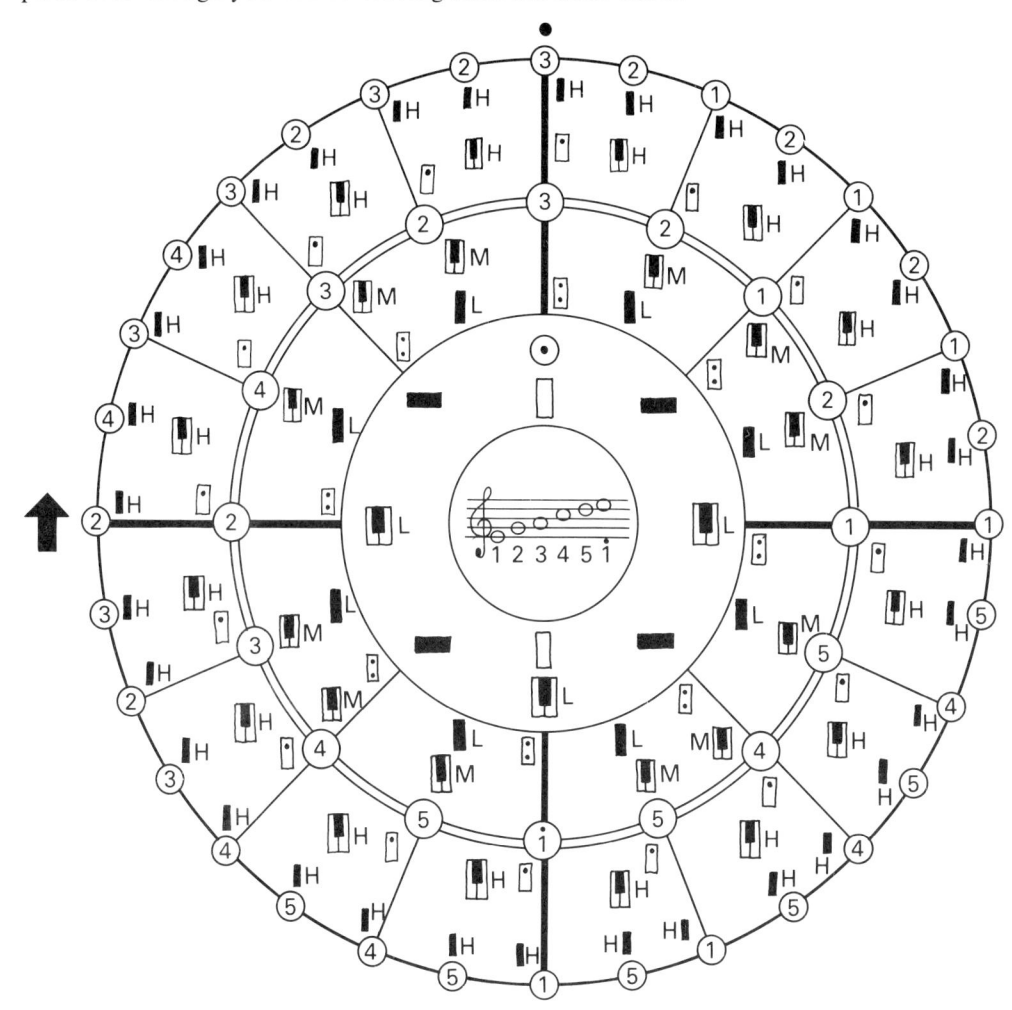

MBIRA

Linguaphone from Zimbabwe

A linguaphone is an instrument which produces a sound by plucking a tongue (*lingua* means tongue in Latin), which is usually made of metal, but may be of wood or shell. African instrument makers have used this idea to produce complicated instruments which may use as many as 52 separate tongues, each playing a different note.

For many years, white settlers in Zimbabwe (which used to be called Rhodesia) insisted on calling the mbira a 'thumb piano'. Modern players resent this name because it suggests that the mbira is an inferior version of a European instrument, whereas it is, in fact, a type of instrument unique to black Africa.

This is why the mbira has become associated with politics in Zimbabwe. During the struggle for democratic government between 1965 and 1980, playing the mbira was recognized as support for the nationalist movement. People put aside their homemade guitars and took up the mbira. Since independence in 1980 the instrument has become a symbol of the new nation. Here is an example of some mbira music which can be played on the piano.

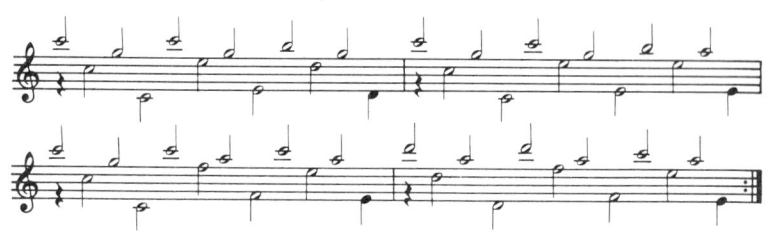

It is difficult to see how such peaceful music can have associations with fighting. This music is supposed to put people in touch with the spirit world. Players say that it makes them 'dreamy, peaceful, calm, unafraid'. When words are sung to mbira accompaniment, they often tell the history of the people of Zimbabwe and of the strength of their ancestors.

It is the relationship with the spirits of the ancestors that gives mbira music its political message. Listening to the mbira gives a sense of belonging to a race with a strong identity and a tradition of independence.

Things to do

1. You can make a simple linguaphone yourself in five seconds by holding a ruler firmly over the edge of a table and hitting the free end. If you make the portion of the ruler sticking out shorter, the sound becomes higher, if you make it longer, it becomes lower.

2. Make a list of instruments which you associate with particular countries. For instance, which countries do you associate with the bagpipe or the harp? How many others can you think of?

Add up all your lists into one huge list, missing out any which the majority of you feel are not quite right.

Linguaphones throughout the world

The marimbula is the Cuban version of the mbira. It is usually very large and deep-toned. It was taken to the Americas by negro slaves and was once widespread but now it only survives in Central and South America.

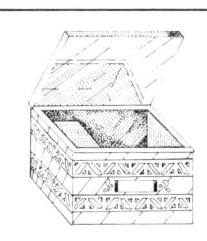

The European musical box developed out of the earlier musical clock in the late 18th century. Very little is known about the origin of the musical box, but it seems likely that it was first made in Switzerland and could have been influenced by African linguaphones which were known in Europe by that time.

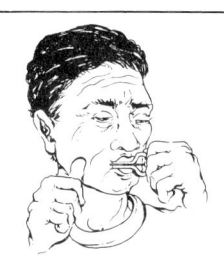

The Jew's harp is not a harp and is not Jewish. It is a linguaphone and it is found throughout Europe and Asia. The player uses the size of his mouth cavity to change the note sounded by the tongue of the instrument.

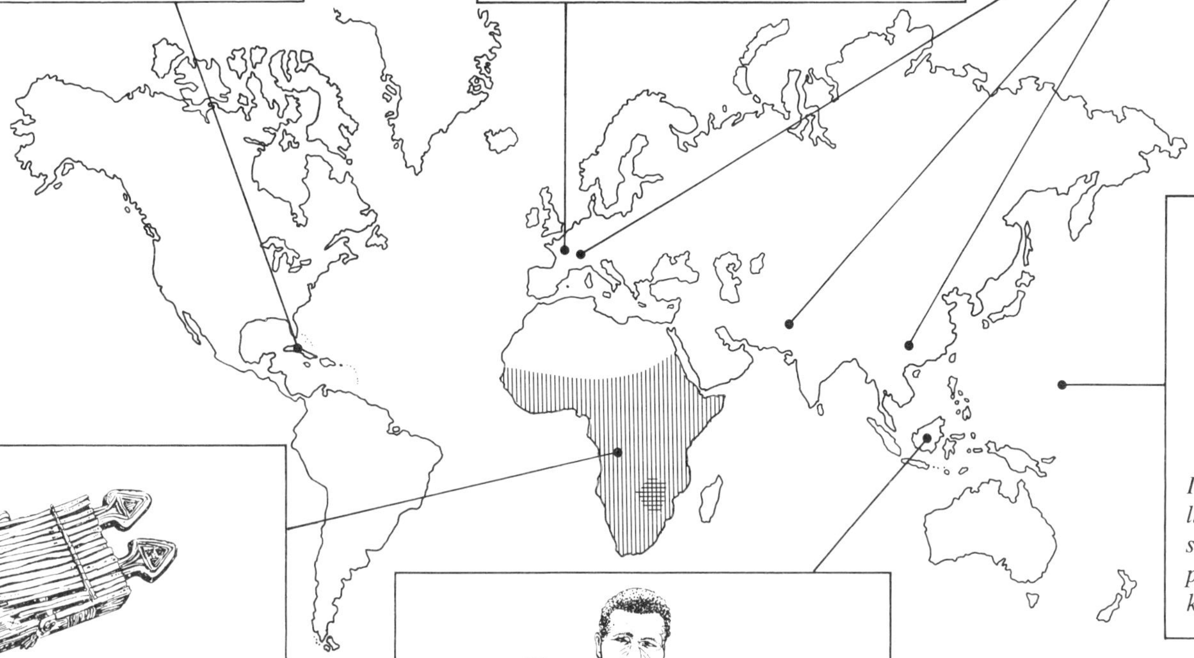

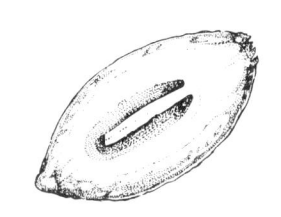

In Melanesia, people make a very simple linguaphone by carving a tongue in the surface of a fruit- or nutshell. The tongue is plucked and the shell acts as a resonator. It is known as cricri.

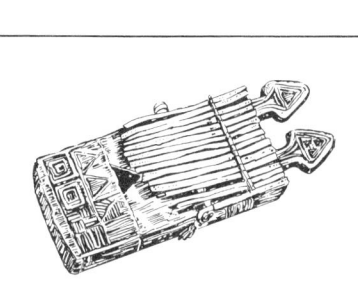

Mbira-like instruments, usually referred to as sanzas, are found in those areas of Africa where the xylophone is also popular. It is possible that the sanza started life as a small, portable version of the xylophone. This sanza from Zaire has tongues of hollowed-out cane filled with seeds to make a rattling sound.

Jew's harps in Borneo are an extension of the Melanesian cricri. The tongue and frame are still cut out of a single piece of wood, but the mouth is used to amplify the sound. It is often associated with courtship.

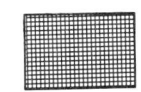

▦ = area covered by the mbira

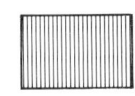

▥ = area in which similar instruments are used

Learning to play the mbira

Mbira players often start to play very young and by the time they are teenagers they may be making money from it. They are usually attracted by the sound of the instrument and its association with religious rituals. This gives the young player a chance to become involved in adult activities from which he might otherwise be excluded.

A young player usually has a teacher. Lessons consist of watching the teacher's fingers on the keys and trying to memorize the piece in that way. Teachers also stress the value of a good memory, strength and endurance. These are necessary for the all-night religious festivals at which mbira players often have to perform.

When the pupil is good enough to start performing, he will play a fixed part while his teacher improvises around it. By taking notice of what his teacher is doing, the student will learn how to 'share ideas with the mbira' himself.

Making an Mbira

YOU WILL NEED
Piece of wood approximately 15 × 10 cm and at least 1.5 cm thick
Metal coat hanger
Nails or heavy duty staples
Hammer
Pliers with cutting edge
File
Anvil or sheet of metal or concrete slab

HOW TO MAKE **Time needed 30 minutes**
Cut two lengths of wire (A and B) from the coat hanger. They should be slightly shorter than the width of the piece of wood. Fix one of these (A) to the wood about 5cm from one end, using a staple at each end of the wire.

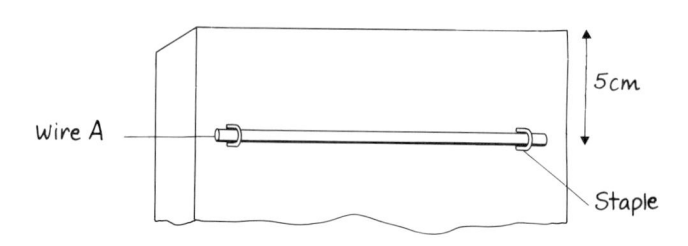

Now cut a further five pieces of wire. Make them all different lengths between 7 and 12 cm. Hammer one end of each of them into a flattened wedge shape, holding them against the anvil or concrete slab with pliers, not with your fingers. Round off the ends with a file.

Fix your keys to the wood by resting them on wire A and securing them with the second length of wire (B), using staples between each key, not just at either end of the wire.

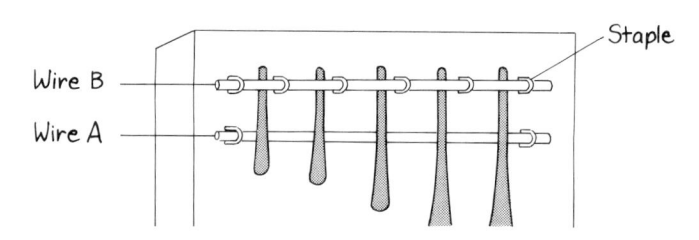

Playing your mbira
Hold the instrument in the palms of both hands with the keys pointing towards you and hit a key with a thumb. If the sound is dull, or buzzy, the most likely fault is that the key is not pressing down on wire A firmly enough. Hammer it down, or bend it slightly until it makes a mellow sound which does not die away quickly.

Do this for each key. You can also tune the keys to whichever notes you want by pushing them in and out: the less key there is pointing over wire A, the higher the note becomes. Adjust all the keys in this way until they all play one of the white notes of the piano. Write the names of the notes your mbira plays on the wood below each key. For instance, one might play D B E G A and another C B D F G.

Now play your mbira using both thumbs. The left thumb plays the two high keys on the left and the right thumb plays the lower three on the right. Alternate thumbs and change keys whenever you like. The sound you make will be a bit like the tune given on page 42, though less complicated.

Playing an mbira inside a metal wastepaper basket or similar container will amplify the sound. Players in Zimbabwe use the dried skins of large gourds.

Playing: Bira

A bira is a social gathering consisting of mbira playing accompanied by percussion instruments and hand-clapping, dancing, beer-drinking, conversation, and ancestor worship which may culminate in one of the participants becoming possessed by a spirit and having revelations. This piece deals only with the musical part of the bira.

Preparation
Split into four groups and practise your parts.

GROUP 1 Hand clappers
Hand clappers are essential to the success of this piece because they give the rhythm which everyone else follows. There are twelve even beats in the rhythm and four separate parts, A, B, C and D. Everyone claps on the first beat, but after that, each part is different. Look at the diagram below:

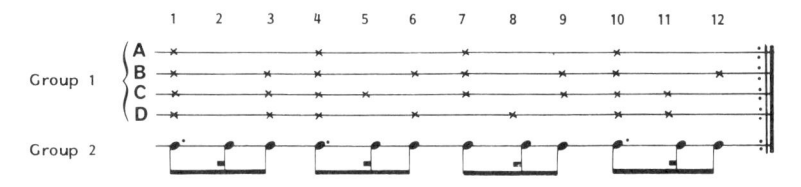

Practise over and over without pausing at beat 12. If each part makes the clap slightly different in tone, (for instance by cupping hands, or clapping against the legs), the result can be an exciting and varied pattern of sound.

GROUP 2 Maracas and other rattles
Make your own rattles from tin cans and stones, or from bottle tops on a string. You repeat one short rhythm all the way through the piece:

When you can play this easily, join group 1 and add your rhythm to theirs. The first beat of your rhythm comes on beats 1, 4, 7 and 10, as in group 1 part A.

GROUP 3 Mbiras and high xylophones
Mbiras helped out by high xylophones play on beats 1, 3, 5, 7, 9, and 11. The notes you play are given below:

1	2	3	4	5	6	7	8	9	10	11	12
G		C		B		C		A		B	

Play whichever notes you have on your instrument. Miss out beats if you do not have a note for them.

GROUP 4 Mbiras, low xylophones and dampened piano
Mbiras, helped out by low xylophones and dampened piano, play in between group 3's notes on beats 2, 4, 6, 8, 10 and 12. Here are your notes:

1	2	3	4	5	6	7	8	9	10	11	12
	C		E		D		C		F		E

As with group 3, miss out beats you do not have a note for.

To play
Group 1 establishes the rhythm. Group 2 joins in. Then groups 3 and 4 come in with the melody. Once the piece has started, keep it going. Concentrate very hard and try to put your notes or claps in exactly the right place. There will be mistakes and this will make the piece more interesting, but the overall effect should be one of trance-like repetition.

A bira

SHENG

Mouth organ from China

The mouth organ was invented in China over 3,000 years ago, but instruments of this type have only been made in the West for the last 200 years. There are two reasons for this. One was that although the Chinese mouth organ gradually spread outside China and eventually found its way into nearly every country in Asia, no examples of the instrument reached Europe until the middle of the 17th century.

The second reason was that even once the instrument was known in Europe, instrument makers were so puzzled by it that they found it nearly impossible to copy. This was because the sheng makes a sound by means of a metal reed moving backwards and forwards inside a closely-fitting frame. This is know as a 'free reed' and it plays the same note whether it is sucked or blown. This method of sound production was completely unknown to European instrument makers and it took them well over a hundred years to imitate it.

Even then, the instruments they made were far from perfect and it was not until the 1820s that German makers began to produce something resembling the modern mouth organ. This instrument can be both sucked and blown like the sheng, but it needs two different reeds for each note to do this whereas the sheng only requires one. So Western technology has still not come up with anything as simple and efficient as the 3,000 year-old Chinese equivalent.

The fact that the sheng was played by sucking in air as well as blowing led to some interesting superstitions about it. In 1882, a Western observer wrote that:

> 'One very rarely hears the sheng nowadays, on account of a curious superstition. The Chinese say that a skilful performer on the sheng becomes so wedded to its music that he is ever playing; but the instrument is played by sucking in the breath, and a long continuance of this brings on inflammation of the bronchial tubes and diseases of the lungs. So no performer is ever known to live longer than forty years.'

This is probably not the main reason for the present unpopularity of the sheng in China. The instrument was always associated with weddings and funerals practised according to Confucian ritual. As these ancient religious customs have died out during the 20th century, especially since the Communist party has ruled China, the sheng found itself less in demand. However, there is now a small revival of interest in the sheng. It no longer plays slow and serious music for religious rituals, but has been adapted to playing the type of modern folk-songs approved of by Chinese politicians, such as the following tune:

Things to do

1. If you have any free-reed instruments, melodicas, harmonicas, concertinas, etc., take off the protective covers and see how they work.
2. Invent a superstition about an instrument you know. It could be about the way it is played, or its shape, or what it is used for in addition to making a noise.

Imagine you are a foreign traveller to this country who has just come across this strange belief. Write a letter to a friend back home describing what the natives, (i.e. us), think about it.

Free-reed instruments throughout the world

In the first half of the 19th century French organ builders combined free reeds with the piano keyboard for an instrument which sounded something like an organ but was much smaller. It was called the harmonium, and became especially popular in America, where it was called the 'American organ'.

The concertina was devised by Charles Wheatstone of London in 1829. It was a variation on the slightly older accordion and was worked by a bellows with boxes of free reeds fitted to either end. This type of instrument was invented too late to become part of the symphony orchestra and has been mainly used for playing folk and popular music.

The harmonica is usually referred to as a mouth organ. It originated in Germany, but is now known everywhere. It is very portable and this has added to its popularity.

The American harmonica player Larry Adler has shown that the instrument can play very complicated music and several composers like Vaughan Williams and Darius Milhaud have written works for him to play.

The Dayak people of Borneo have a sheng-like instrument with reeds made out of bamboo called a kledi.

The melodica is the most modern development of the mouth organ and is popular with children because it is very easy to play.

▦ = area covered by the sheng

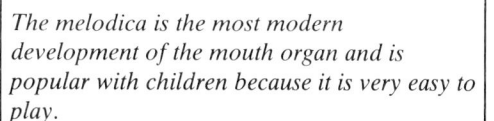

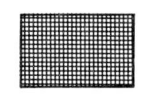

▦ = area in which similar instruments are used

The khen from Laos has reeds made out of silver. It comes in three sizes and the largest may have pipes up to three metres long.

47

Listening

Record cover to 'Tin Drum', by Japan

Japan are a modern British group whose music shows the influence of many non-European musical styles. Their album *Tin Drum* has three tracks on it with strong references to China; *Visions of China*, *Cantonese Boy* and the instrumental *Canton*. *Canton* uses a synthesizer to make a sound very like the sheng. It plays a melody which is in many respects similar to the sheng tune on page 46:

Both tunes start by moving up to their highest notes and end on their lowest note. Both pause on a long note in the middle of the tune. This note is between the highest and the lowest notes used. They have unexpectedly wide gaps between some of the notes instead of moving in step from one note to the next.

Music of Changes by John Cage

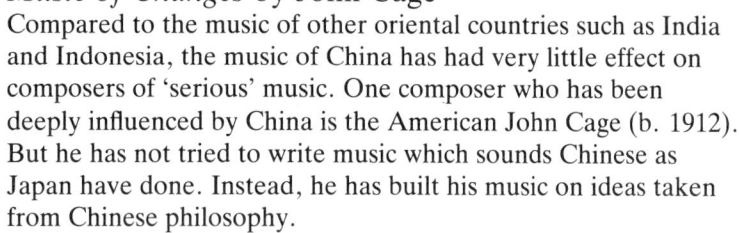

Compared to the music of other oriental countries such as India and Indonesia, the music of China has had very little effect on composers of 'serious' music. One composer who has been deeply influenced by China is the American John Cage (b. 1912). But he has not tried to write music which sounds Chinese as Japan have done. Instead, he has built his music on ideas taken from Chinese philosophy.

Zen Buddhism teaches that everything does not necessarily happen according to logic and that there is not an answer to every question. It also suggests that the Earth is here to be enjoyed, not to be analysed and commented on.

John Cage

This led Cage to believe that it was useless to write music which tried to put sounds into any particular order, and that one sound was as good as another for listening to. So one of his pieces makes use of the random tunings of 12 radio sets, and another consists entirely of silence (or, to be more accurate, the sounds you hear when you think you are being silent).

Cage's *Music of Changes* has to be performed using methods from the ancient Chinese *Book of Changes* (the *I Ching*). This book is consulted by the Chinese when they have any sort of problem. It does not so much predict the future as suggest ways of behaving in order to bring present problems to a satisfactory conclusion. In the same way, the performer of *Music of Changes* works out which notes to play by tossing three coins six times. The music actually looks quite ordinary:

Although the notes played in any performance of this piece will always be the same, every performance will sound different because the order of the notes is arrived at by chance.

Learning to play the sheng

Nowadays, a Chinese child who wishes to play music will probably learn Western music. Traditional Chinese instruments are still played on mainland China, but the music they are expected to play is heavily influenced by Western ideas and all instruments have had to adapt to playing the type of music dictated by the authorities.

This means that modern Chinese music is more likely to be based on folk and popular music than on classical or religious music. So instruments such as the sheng which were mainly for religious use have not been in favour in recent years.

But the situation is now changing yet again and traditional classical music is once more being played in China, though it is still overshadowed by the Western and folk-influenced styles.

This means that if you wanted to learn to play the sheng, it would not be much use going to China. You would be better off in Hong Kong, Taiwan or America, where Chinese communities have maintained their traditional cultures and it is possible for Westerners to learn Chinese music. Here is a photograph of American university students playing in a Chinese orchestra.

American students playing Chinese music

Music and politics in China

There have been several mentions of the way politics affects music in China. This is not a modern trend. The Chinese have always believed that music is closely connected with the practicalities of life. In the time of Confucius (6th century B.C.) it was thought necessary to understand music in order to know how to govern a country.

In the 14th century, there were different types of music for the different social classes and it was considered dangerous to listen to music which was designed for another class. This might lead to civil war.

Now, music is seen as a way of educating people to accept communist ideals and creating a sense of unity. Music is meant to serve the masses, so there are no 'star' performers or composers. In fact, composers are often not even given the credit for the pieces they write because music belongs to the people, not to individuals. One of the most interesting developments in Chinese music is that composers often work in groups rather than on their own. These 'composers' collectives' share work and profit in the same way as groups of factory workers or farmers.

Playing exercises

Form a 'singers' collective' and learn to sing the tune on page 46. When you know it well, split into six groups and number yourselves from 1 to 6.

Sing the tune again, but this time, do not all sing together. Group 1 sings the first note, group 2 the second note, group 3 the third, etc. And so on until the tune is finished.

This is not as easy as it sounds. It is especially difficult to keep the rhythm moving at an even speed.

You can have a lot of fun singing in this way. Try other tunes you all know.

Making a mouth organ

The sheng is a delicate instrument and the free reed is very difficult to make. The instrument on this page is made in a slightly different way to the sheng, but it makes a similar sound and is more robust.

YOU WILL NEED
A plastic carton (type used for yoghurt, cream or glacé fruit)
Cardboard, plastic or wooden tubes (Smartie packets, pen casing, garden cane, etc.)
A plastic bottle
Sellotape
Plasticine
A very sharp knife

HOW TO MAKE **Time needed 30 minutes**
Cut three sides of a small rectangle (about 2 × 8 mm) into the side of the plastic carton to produce a small reed still attached by one short side. Then shave a tiny sliver of plastic off all three sides of the reed so that it flaps freely in the hole left by it.

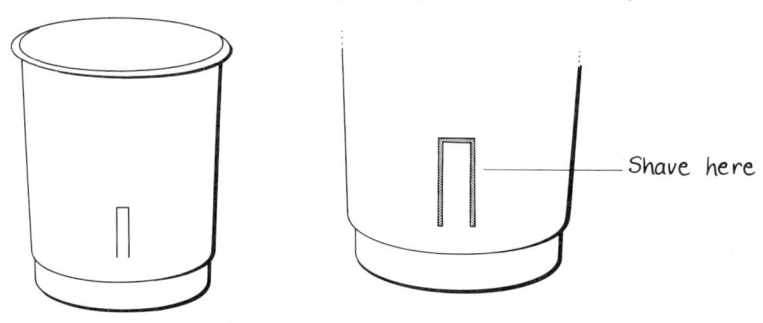

Put your lips onto the carton side, completely surrounding the reed and blow. If this does not make a sound, shave a little plastic off the base of the reed. Keep shaving the reed until a steady tone is produced when you blow. You should not need to blow hard with this type of reed.

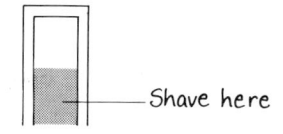

Cut the piece of plastic containing the reed from the carton. Then take your resonating tube and cut a hole near the bottom which is slightly smaller than the piece of plastic. Sellotape the piece of plastic over the hole and seal off the bottom end of the tube.

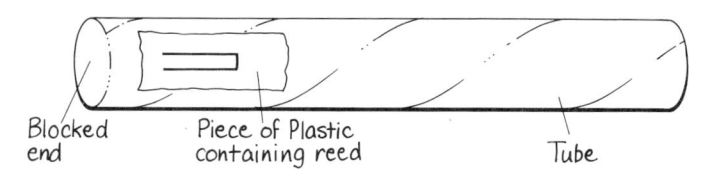

When you blow, the tone should be stronger than before. Make several of these pipes with reeds of slightly different sizes and they will each play a different note.

The plastic bottle is going to be the 'wind chest'. Make holes at opposite sides of the bottle the same size as your tubes. Put the tubes through so that the reeds are inside the bottle. Stop air leaking out of the holes in the bottle by pressing plasticine into the space around the tubes.

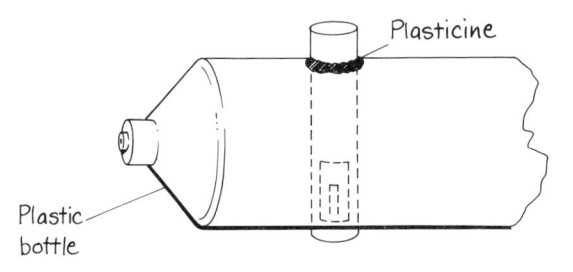

Playing your sheng
To play, simply blow into the open end of the plastic bottle. Obviously, all the reeds will sound at once and you will have to devise a way of silencing those you do not want. A finger over the end of the tube will do. Or if this is difficult whilst holding the instrument as well, cut a hole in the tube near to the bottle and seal off the open end. It will be easier to place a finger over this hole whilst holding the bottle.

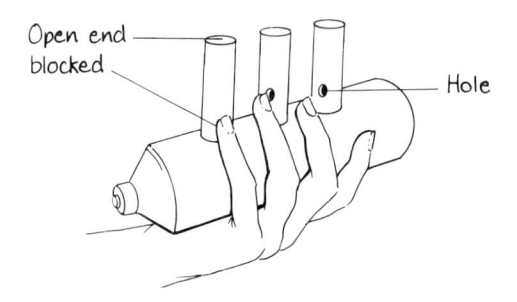

You should now be able to play single notes or chords. In Chinese music, the mouth organ is one of the few instruments which can play chords.

Playing: Music of Chances

This is a piece based on chance in a similar way to John Cage's *Music of Changes*, but using the sound of free-reed instruments and bits of tunes from China. Music which is put together by chance is called aleatoric music, after the Latin word 'alea' which means 'dice'.

Preparation

Split into three groups. In addition, you will need two 'callers' who direct the order of events.

THE CALLERS

The callers make ten large cards. Four are circles, four are diamond-shaped, two are square. Colour one each of the circular and diamond cards red, blue, green and yellow. Colour one of the square cards black and the other white. Put all the cards in a large container.

GROUP 1   Mouth organs, melodicas, recorders

Anyone who can put four or five notes together on a mouth organ, melodica, recorder or any other instrument joins this group. You split into four sections A, B, C and D. Each section learns to play one bar of the tune on page 46. It does not matter if you cannot play exactly in rhythm together, but you should try. Add extra notes to fill out the melody if you wish.

GROUP 2   Homemade mouth organs, electric organs, synthesizers

Use these and any other instruments which make a 'reedy' sound which can be held on for a long time. Split up into four sections A, B, C and D. Each section works out a chord which they like the sound of. Put the chord together note by note, changing those you are not satisfied with. Work at playing the chord for a very long time without any changes in the volume of any of the notes.

GROUP 3   Gongs, suspended cymbals, wood blocks, bells, chime bars

Practise playing in two ways:

1. Everyone plays a single, loud note on their instrument. Try to play at the same time by following the arm movements of one person. Let the sound of all the instruments ring on.

2. Everyone repeats their notes, very quietly for a scattered effect. Listen hard to each other when playing in this way. Try to use your own instrument to make the overall sound as varied and interesting as possible.

To play

Everyone must learn to recognize the coloured card which tells them when to play:

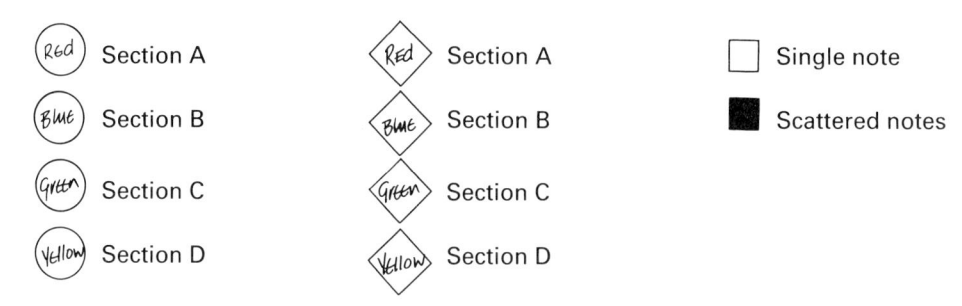

(Red) circle Section A	(Red) diamond Section A	☐	Single note
(Blue) circle Section B	(Blue) diamond Section B	■	Scattered notes
(Green) circle Section C	(Green) diamond Section C		
(Yellow) circle Section D	(Yellow) diamond Section D		

The callers hold up the cards one by one to make sure each group and section is playing when they see their own card. Then all the cards are put into the container.

The performance begins when one of the callers pulls a card out of the container and holds it up. Both callers might hold up cards at the same time, or even hold up two cards each, which would result in a full sound. For instance, if the red circle, the yellow diamond and the black square were held up together, the sound would consist of group 1A playing a snatch of melody, group 2D playing their own chord and group 3 making scattered percussion sounds. On the other hand, the callers might pull out all four circular cards which would lead to four different bits of melody being played at the same time.

Group 1 can play their melodies just once, or repeat them until their card is put back into the container.

The callers continue changing the cards until they feel the piece has gone on for long enough. When they put the last card back in the container, the piece is over.

PEYOTE WATER DRUM

Kettledrum from North America

Most people who have listened to the water drum of the American Indians have commented on its remarkable carrying power. Close to, it sounds rather dull, and not particularly loud, but it can still be heard at considerable distances, sounding just as loud. It is probably this which has led to the drum being associated with magic and medicine, and more recently with religion.

Water drums may be made of pottery, wood or metal. Although they originated in a fairly small area of the southwestern United States among the Apache, Hopi, Pueblo and Navajo tribes, they can now be found from Canada down to Mexico because of their use in the ceremonies of the Native American Church. This religion is a mixture of old Indian beliefs and Christianity and is often referred to as the peyote religion (pronounced *pay-oh-day*) because believers eat a cactus called peyote in their rituals. The cactus acts as a drug on the eaters and causes them to see things differently. They often have brilliantly colourful visions and believe that they have seen Jesus Christ or one of their ancestors.

This probably accounts for the rather glazed expression on the face of the Oklahoma peyote drummer pictured above. He is playing a drum made of iron.

Oklahoma peyote drummer playing a drum made of iron

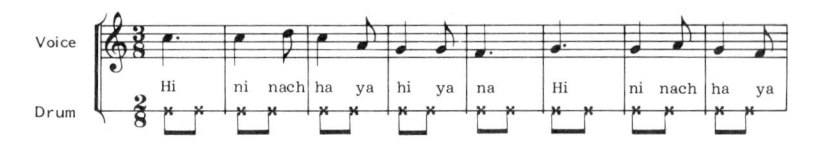

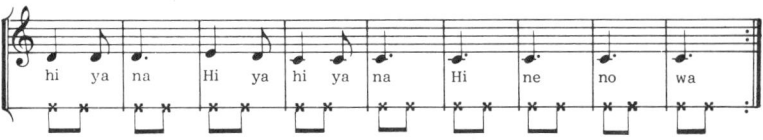

In this peyote song, the drum beat does not always fit in with the rhythm of the song. Even when dancing, American Indians will often beat their drums in completely different rhythms to that of the singing. They seem to be able to carry on two or even three rhythms at the same time, completely independently of each other.

Another interesting thing about this song is that the words are meaningless except to the people who sing them in the peyote ritual. Outsiders are not allowed to understand them. Such words, called vocables, are used in most peyote songs and in many other types of American Indian song also.

Things to do

1. Many American Indian songs use speech rhythms. That is, the length of the notes is determined by the word which is sung to it, not by the musical beat as in most of our songs. However, these songs are accompanied by a regular pulse on the drum. To do this, you have to think in two rhythms at once.

Tap quite fast and absolutely evenly on a desk with a pencil. Now try to carry on a normal conversation or make a short speech. You will probably find that your speech changes to fit in with the beat, or that the beat hesitates. To overcome this, think of the pencil tapping not as a rhythm but as a background sound like the drone of traffic or the patter of rain on a roof.

2. Write a few lines describing the peyote drummer above. Describe his dress and what he is doing. Put in some of the things you now know about this man and his music after re-reading this page.

Kettledrums throughout the world

South American kettledrums are most often made of clay. Like the peyote drum, they can be filled with water.

Naqqara were brought back from the Middle East by the Crusaders. These early nakers, as they were called in Europe, developed into the modern timpani.

Kettledrums have always been associated with the display of wealth and power. They are still played in military processions, carried either side of a horse.

The Arabic naqqara is the parent of all Asian, African and European kettledrums. It originated in Persia in about 600 A.D. making it one of the youngest types of drum.

The Venda people of Southern Africa make kettledrums by stretching a skin over a dried gourd with the top cut off. This huge ngoma is usually played by women.

India has a wide variety of kettledrums. The wooden tudum is carried with a cord and hit with wedge-shaped beaters.
The ceremonial naubat may be as large as 1.5 m in diameter and have to be carried by elephant.
The tabla are a pair of drums used in Indian classical music. The larger, left-hand drum, called baya, is a kettledrum made of metal.

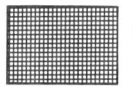

= original distribution of water drum

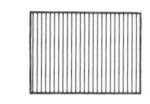

= present day distribution of water drum used in peyote religion

Learning to play in an American Indian tribe

American Indian children learn music by copying what they hear. They soon become very good at this, and some American Indians claim to be able to reproduce a song perfectly after only one hearing. As getting a song 'right' is often considered essential to the success of a ritual, having a quick and reliable memory is a very important part of being a musician. All American Indians are musicians and those who are most highly respected are usually those with the largest number of songs in their repertoire.

American Indians rarely make up new songs. Instead, they claim to receive them in dreams or visions. Teenagers are sometimes sent into the wilderness on these 'song quests' as part of becoming accepted as an adult member of the tribe. Wandering through the desert for days and nights, often without food or drink, it is not surprising that their way of thinking changes and they see and hear some very unusual things. It is then that the ability to memorize quickly enables them to take back a song which will become their own property.

Making a Water Drum

YOU WILL NEED
A plastic, pottery or metal bowl or pot (it is best if it has a lip on it, but any bowl, of any size will do). The bigger the bowl, the deeper the sound.
A piece of cloth (an old cotton or linen sheet is ideal). It must be larger than the top of your bowl.
A piece of string at least 10 times longer than the circumference of your bowl
Water

HOW TO MAKE   **Time needed 10 minutes**
Fill your bowl about one quarter full of water, and soak the cloth in it. Wring out the cloth and put it over the top of the bowl. Now tie a small loop at one end of the string, leaving about 3 cm of string after the loop. Be careful to stop your string getting tangled.

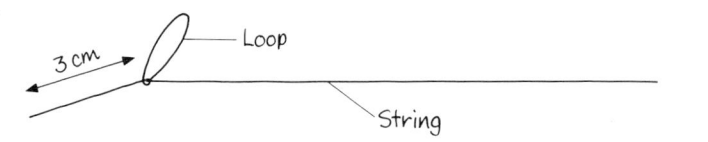

Now thread the long end of the string through the loop to make a noose. Place this over the drum head and pull tight.

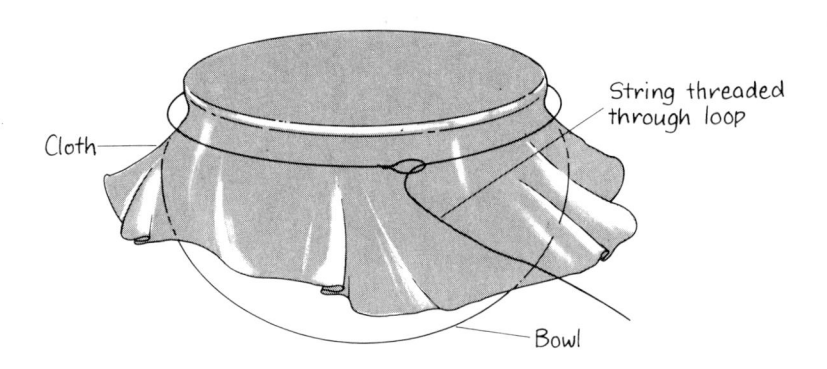

Wrap the string around the top of the bowl several times always making sure you are holding it as tightly as possible. After four or five turns, tie a knot against the bowl using the two ends of the string. Pull the loose cloth all around the bowl to tighten up the drum head. Wrap around the remainder of the string and tie tightly.

Playing your drum
Using a wooden stick, hit the drum head repeatedly at a fast but even speed. American Indians do not use drums to keep the rhythm but to create a backcloth of sound against which songs and dances take place, so do not create a beat by making some notes louder than others.

It may seem strange to say that a water drum can make a 'dry' sound, but the tone of your drum should have very little resonance. This is because the water on the drum head prevents what are called overtones, those high sounds which most instruments use to make their tone fuller and more interesting. All you hear is the lowest or 'fundamental' note of the drum head. The water inside the drum actually makes very little difference to the final sound.

Experiment by making some drums without water, but with a water-soaked drum head, and others with a dry head. Compare the sound they make.

You can also test the legendary carrying power of these drums by walking away from the room where they are being played until the sound disappears.

Playing: Moccasin Game

Indians love games, and Indian games, like many of our own, are often accompanied by music. In the Moccasin game, one team hides a pebble in one of the four moccasins laid in a row and the other team tries to guess where the pebble is. Meanwhile, songs are sung and drums are played to put off the guessers. Such songs are often highly insulting and are sung in a taunting manner.

Your version of the Moccasin game acts out an American Indian myth. Day and night are having an argument over who should be the longest. To settle the matter, they resort to a game of chance. Whoever wins the game will be longest.

Of course, if any game of chance is played for long enough, both sides will eventually be equal, just as wherever you live in the world, day and night are the same length if you measure them over a whole year. This is the moral of the mythological story: to show that day and night, as all things in nature, must be in balance.

Preparation

Divide into two equal groups. Each group splits into instrumentalists and singers.

GROUP 1 Drums and singers

Instruments: Drums of all types, shapes and sizes, including water drums. Practise playing your drums to an even beat which never changes, as you did on the previous page.

Singers learn this melody:

Make sure you can sing this to the accompaniment of the drumming without changing the rhythm of your singing.

A pilgrim of the Huichol tribe searching for the peyote cactus

Next, everyone gets together to make up words which praise your own side or insult the opposition. The words must fit the rhythm of your melody. Group 1 represents night, so they might sing:

The night sky is very beau–ti–ful,
Stars and moon give light e–nough for us.

You need to have a good supply of words as the game can go on for some time. Write them down so that you do not forget them. Accompany these songs on recorders to help find the notes.

GROUP 2 Rasps, rattles, wood blocks, bells, clappers, maracas and singers

Two rulers held together and hit against a desk are effective clappers. Practise playing a consistent background sound in the same way as group 1.

Singers learn this melody:

Like group 1, you make up words to your melody, but from the point of view of the day. For instance, you might mock night like this:

Hide all day, out of sight.
Too ug–ly to be seen.

To play

You need a referee. Make two large cards, one black and one white. You also need a watch with a second hand and a coin. Toss the coin. If it comes down heads, hold up the white card, if it comes down tails, hold up the black card. Time 10 seconds, during which you toss the coin again. At the end of the 10 seconds, hold up the appropriate card.

If the black card is held up, then group 1 plays drums and sings. If the white card is shown, group 2 play their instruments and sing. You may need to play for several sets of 10 seconds one after the other depending on the way the coin falls, so be prepared to go on.

The piece finishes when the referee decides that both groups have had an equal chance to state their case and does not hold up the cards any longer. Both groups then play together for about 30 seconds (the tunes go together surprisingly well) until the referee signals end of play by holding up a yellow card.

HARDANGER FIDDLE

Folk violin from Norway

The Hardanger fiddle looks nothing like the plain brown violin, though it is basically the same instrument underneath all the ornamentation. Some of the carving and painting on it, such as the peg box in the shape of a lion with a gilt crown, go back to Viking times. But the instrument is much more recent. It was invented in 1670 in Hardanger on the west coast of Norway and is still played mainly in that area of the country.

Although it is very similar to the violin played in orchestras, there are some differences in construction which make it more suited to playing the sort of music it is used for. The neck is shorter because folk fiddle players do not need to play the high notes that classical violinists are sometimes expected to. The strings are all at nearly the same height from the fingerboard so that players can play several strings at the same time if they wish.

But the main difference between the Hardanger fiddle and the classical violin is that it has extra strings running underneath the neck of the instrument which are not played with the bow but vibrate in sympathy with the melody notes played on the strings above. Sympathetic strings, as they are called, are virtually unknown in other European countries but are often found in instruments from India (there is some information and an experiment on this on page 30 of this book).

Hardanger fiddle players are very fond of the full sound given by these extra strings and emphasize this by filling out their melodies still further by adding drone notes and rudimentary second tunes on the strings below those playing the main melody.

Like the instrument, the music is heavily ornamented. It is also in an unusual rhythm with irregular numbers of beats to each bar. This is even more strange when you realize that this is dance music and what most dancers require from their musicians is a strong and regular beat. Hardanger fiddle players usually make up for this by stamping their foot heavily as they play. It is one of the hallmarks of the style of this music that the melodies cut across the rhythm of the dances they accompany rather than assist in keeping the beat.

Things to do

1. Make a violin with a chair and two pieces of string. Tie one piece of string very tightly between the legs of the chair. It should make a dull but reasonably resonant note if you pluck it. Rub violin bow rosin on the second piece of string. Hold this piece tightly between your two hands and rub against the first piece in a sawing motion. It should sound like a deep and muted violin.

2. Your town has arranged an exchange visit with a town in Norway and as part of their visit, the Norwegian guests are putting on an evening of traditional folk music and dance. Design a poster for this event.

Fiddles throughout the world

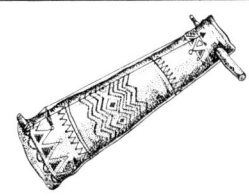

Stringed instruments, especially those played with a bow are virtually unknown to Indians in North and South America. One of the few exceptions is the 'Apache fiddle' made from a hollowed out cactus stem and strings of horsehair. It is inspired by the European violin, although it looks nothing like it.

The double bass is the largest member of the violin family. It is used in orchestras, where it is usually played with a bow, in jazz bands, where it is usually plucked and in folk music groups, especially in Eastern Europe.

The Mongolian morinxur is associated with horses. It has a horse's head carved at the top of the neck and plays music filled with galloping rhythms and sounds imitating neighing and whinnying.

In India, stringed instruments played with a bow are thought to be closer to the human voice than any other instrument, so they are often used to accompany singing. In South India, they play the European violin, held with the peg box resting on the player's foot. But in North India the favoured instrument is the sarangi.

As well as spreading east to Java, the rebab spread south into Africa. In Ethiopia it changed from having a round body to a square one and became called the masenquo.

The rebab is an Arabic instrument which has spread to many parts of the world with the spread of the Muslim religion. In Java, the rebab is normally the only stringed instrument in the gamelan which mainly consists of xylophones and gongs.

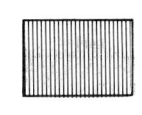

= area covered by the Hardanger fiddle

57

Listening

Edvard Grieg

Edvard Grieg (1843–1907) was a Norwegian composer who was deeply influenced by his native folk music. For most of his life, Norway was politically joined to Sweden and culturally under the shadow of Denmark and Germany. Writing music which sounded Norwegian was a way of expressing his desire for an independent Norway, which came about in 1905, two years before his death.

Norwegian composers and folk-song collectors before Grieg had started to let the concert-going public know about Norwegian folk music, but Grieg was the first composer who succeeded in combining the sounds of his country with music which belonged to the mainstream of European composition. He was the first Norwegian composer to gain recognition outside his own country and is still one of the best known Scandinavian composers.

Violin Sonata No. 1 in F

Grieg wrote his first violin sonata when he was a young man studying music in Germany. Most of the composition is in the accepted style of the day, strongly influenced by the music of Schumann and Wagner, but in the second movement, Grieg introduces a tune obviously taken from folk-dance music.

A few bars later, he gives us the unmistakable sound of the Hardanger fiddle:

Grieg's writing for the violin is not as complicated as the piece of genuine Hardanger fiddle music given on page 56. After all, this was written for classical violinists who would not be familiar with the style. Also, he would have to simplify the rhythm as the violin is accompanied by a piano, and in 1865 (when the sonata was written), musicians were not trained to play together in such a way as to cope with changes of rhythm between bars. It is also possible that Grieg actually thought that Norwegian folk music did fit into the same rhythms as European art music. It is not unusual for people to hear music not as it really sounds, but as they think it ought to sound according to their training.

Other works

Once you know the distinctly Norwegian sounds of drones, dance-like rhythms, and small melodic fragments repeated with small variations, you will be able to hear them in other pieces by Grieg. The opening tune to the finale of his famous piano concerto has all these characteristics.

But his best known composition must be the incidental music composed for Ibsen's play *Peer Gynt*. The play is about a Norwegian who travels abroad and gets himself into all sorts of trouble because he is searching for something, he is not sure what, to give meaning to his life. Meanwhile, his true love Solveig waits for him to return and sings a song which conjures up a picture of rural Norway.

Notice how similar this tune is to the first tune from the violin sonata even though it is much slower and does not use a dance-rhythm. The accompaniment consists of a drone bass and simple chords and the tune itself is mainly made up of one musical phrase repeated on lower notes.

It is followed by a brighter, dancing figure which also uses a drone and has all the other hallmarks of Norwegian folk music. By the time Grieg wrote *Peer Gynt*, folk music had become so much a part of the way he composed that it is no longer possible to hear the joins where his 'European' style ends and his 'Norwegian' style begins.

Learning to play folk music

Methods of learning to play folk music in Norway are much the same as in the rest of Western Europe. There is little formal training; musicians usually pick up the tunes and style by listening to older players. They may also listen to records and sometimes use written music as a way of getting to know individual tunes.

These days, classically-trained violinists often learn to play Hardanger fiddle and other folk-fiddle styles. This has led to an extension in the type of music played and some development of the techniques used, but the people who use this music for dancing and listening to do not accept changes quickly. Close contact with the style over a long period is the only way to be sure of playing in such a way that knowledgeable listeners will accept the sound as belonging to the tradition.

The style and sound of the Hardanger fiddle has been exported to Britain. If you look at a map of North Western Europe, you will see that the Shetland Isles, which are English-speaking and politically part of the United Kingdom, are nearer to Norway than to mainland Britain. For centuries, when water was the main means of communication, the people of the Shetland Isles had more in common with Norwegians than with the Scots or English.

There is still a lot of evidence of this old relationship in Shetland, mainly in the names of people and places, and in fiddle music. This music is based very closely on the sound and style of Norwegian folk music, but the Hardanger fiddle itself, with its sympathetic strings and elaborate decoration is only very rarely found on Shetland.

Playing exercise

You are going to tackle some of the complicated rhythms used in Norwegian folk music. First set up a regular foot-stamping, not too fast: a little slower than one stamp per second. Now add two taps with your other foot between the stamps. These taps should not be of quite equal length; the second is slightly longer. The effect is that the rhythm drags slightly towards the end. Do this until you no longer need to concentrate to keep the rhythm accurately.

Now practise clapping on each of the three beats in turn. The stamping beat is easy. But clapping on either of the two taps is more difficult.

Next you are going to make up patterns of clapping to fit in with your foot-beats. Here is one to get you started. Then try others.

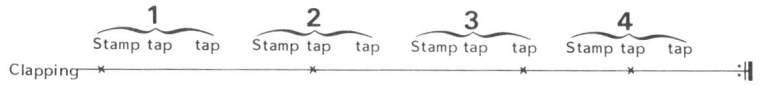

Shetland Fiddle Band

Making a folk fiddle

The Hardanger fiddle is a complicated instrument made in a similar way to the violin and it is not possible to make an instrument like this without special tools. But many European countries also have folk fiddles of much simpler construction.

YOU WILL NEED
A cardboard box (washing powder box is ideal)
A piece of dowel or broom handle about 70 cm long
Ruler about 35 cm
1 m of 15 amp fuse wire
Short piece of thick wire (piece of coat hanger)
2 small screws • 1 screw hook
Corrugated cardboard (small piece)
Sellotape • Sharp knife • Screwdriver

HOW TO MAKE   **Time needed 40 minutes**

Cut holes in the top and bottom of your cardboard box the same size as your dowel rod. Place them centrally but close to the front face of the box. Push the dowel rod through so that it protrudes about 5 cm from the bottom of the box. Fix firmly with Sellotape.

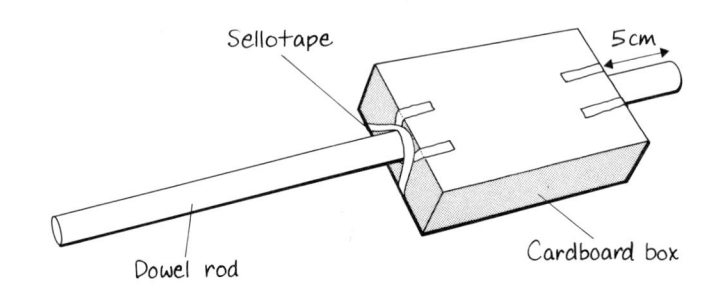

Now sellotape the ruler to the long piece of dowel so that it overlaps the box by 4 cm or 5 cm.

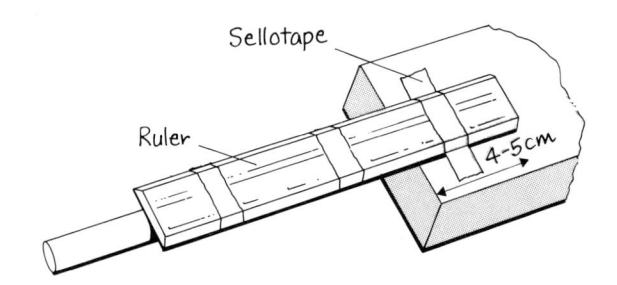

Make a short triangular tube out of the piece of corrugated cardboard: Cut it to about 6 × 4 cm (with the corrugations running lengthways). Score one side of the cardboard into three equal sections.

Fold the cardboard into a triangle. Fix with Sellotape. This is the bridge.

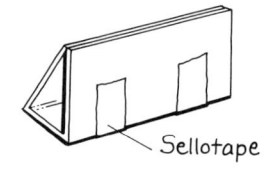

Sellotape the length of thick wire near the top of the ruler.

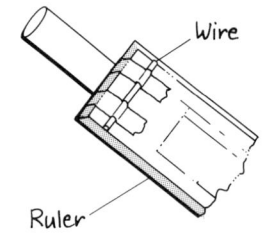

Place a screw near to each end of the dowel rod, facing the front. Screw the hook into one side of the dowel rod near the top. Leave about one quarter of the thread showing.

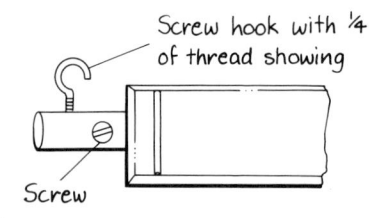

Tie one end of the fuse wire firmly to the screw hook and wrap around a few times so that it will not slip. Now pass it round the far side of the nearest screw and tie it tightly to the screw at the other end of the dowelling. Raise the string off the ruler by pushing the cardboard bridge under it near the bottom of the box.

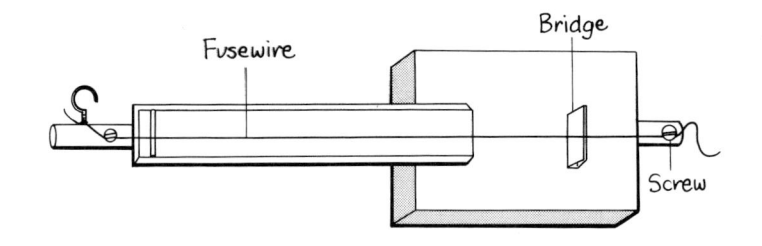

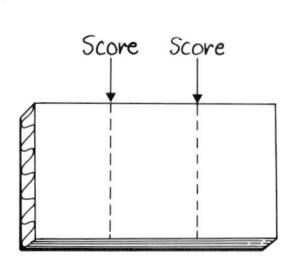

Playing your folk fiddle

Place the fiddle on your left shoulder and under your chin like a violin and use a well-rosined violin bow held in the right hand to make the string sound. If the string is too loose, tighten it by turning the screw hook to take up the slack.

Once you can get a good sound on the string, try playing different notes by placing your left-hand fingers on the string along the ruler. Use the markings on the ruler to remember combinations of notes which make up well-known tunes or to create your own melodies.

If you do not have a violin bow, you can make one out of a piece of thick elastic fixed to either end of a curved stick. Several lengths of thick wool will also make a bow, but the sound will not be as full as with a violin bow made from horsehair.

Playing: Sympathetic Strings

This piece uses the idea of strings vibrating in sympathy with one another, but instead of being attached to the same instrument and picking up the vibrations from the melody strings, they are played by you on separate instruments.

Preparation

Split into three groups.

GROUP 1 Violin, recorder, piano

Anyone who can play a few notes on a violin or recorder joins this group. You can also use the piano with the damper pedal down.

The group divides into two sections. Section A learns to play this tune:

Section B learns this tune:

Better players can learn both tunes if they wish.

Choose a leader who will tell you which tune to play by shouting out 'A' or 'B'. Practise playing one tune several times and then changing to the second tune without a break and without changing the speed of playing.

GROUP 2 Homemade folk-fiddles, guitars, violins, cellos, etc.

You do not need to be able to play the instrument properly as you are only going to play open notes. Do not bother to tune the instruments.

Practise playing very quietly. If you are not used to using a bow it may take some time to be able to make a pleasant sound with it. If you are plucking your instrument, play very softly with the flesh of your fingers. Listen carefully to the notes the different strings play.

GROUPS 1 AND 2

Groups 1 and 2 then practise together. Group 1 play the melodies and help group 2 to identify any notes in the melodies which they are able to play on their open strings. Next, group 1 play the melodies very slowly and group 2 join in, very quietly, on any notes they can play and hold the note on until they hear it played again.

GROUP 3 Stampers and clappers

You are the stampers and clappers who keep the rhythm and add the atmosphere. Practise the exercise given on page 59. This is the basic rhythm for the piece and you must be able to play it without hesitation. Add whoops and yells at any point in the manner of folk-dancers if you want.

To play

Group 3 establish the rhythm. The leader of group 1 brings in tune A at the beginning of a rhythmic cycle, (where the stamp and the clap come together). Group 1 repeat tune A several times and group 2 add the sympathetic resonance on their open strings.

The leader then signals to change tunes and the sympathetic strings change as well to create a very different sound.

The piece goes on alternating between tunes A and B until the leader shouts 'Finish next time'. On the completion of the next tune and rhythmic cycle, everyone stops playing.

Around the world in 80 bars

This final piece is a combination of all the previous pieces in the book, joined together by sounds which suggest travelling to the different countries.

There are 13 different methods of transport. The sounds associated with them are very simple to produce, so you can all make all of them if there are enough instruments to go round. Practise playing all 13 now and learn to recognize the diagram which identifies each sound.

MOTORBIKE
Mouth noises imitating motorbike going up through gears. Trumpet or other high brass instrument for the horn.

HORSE
Wood block or coconut shells making 'clip-clop'. Guitar or piano adds:

ROCKET
Bass drum or kettledrums for take off. Chime bars, triangles, glockenspiels, etc. for outer space.

REINDEER
Bells. Wire brush on a gong for the sleigh. Sing *Rudolph the Red-nosed Reindeer*.

TRAIN
Maracas and rattles for rhythm of the wheels:

Whistles and steam whistles on recorders.

ELEPHANT
Plodding rhythm on double bass or bottom strings of the guitar and low drums. Sing *Nellie the Elephant*.

RICKSHAW
Running footsteps. Rasps and rattles for the sound of wheels on rough roads.

SUBMARINE
Blowing bubbles into a bottle with a straw. Sing *We All Live in a Yellow Submarine*.

AEROPLANE
Humming through paper on combs for the humming of the engine. High notes on violins sliding upwards to suggest ascent.

HOT-AIR BALLOON
Blowing into recorder mouthpieces, bottles, pen tops, etc. Brush finger over high strings of an opened-up piano.

SHIP
Foghorn on horn, trombone or other low brass. Wire brushes on snare drum and suspended cymbals for water.

MOTORCAR
Flutter-tonguing into mouth organs. Mouth noises imitating engine.

ROWING BOAT
Water in a bucket and a ruler.

To play
Start wherever you want to on the map opposite. Play the piece associated with the country you are in. Then move in either direction along the dotted line to the next country and piece, playing your travel music as you go. Continue like this until you arrive back where you started.

A full performance of this piece would take between 20 and 30 minutes. You could make up your own journey around fewer countries if you wish.

Happy travelling!

Playing: Around the world in 80 bars

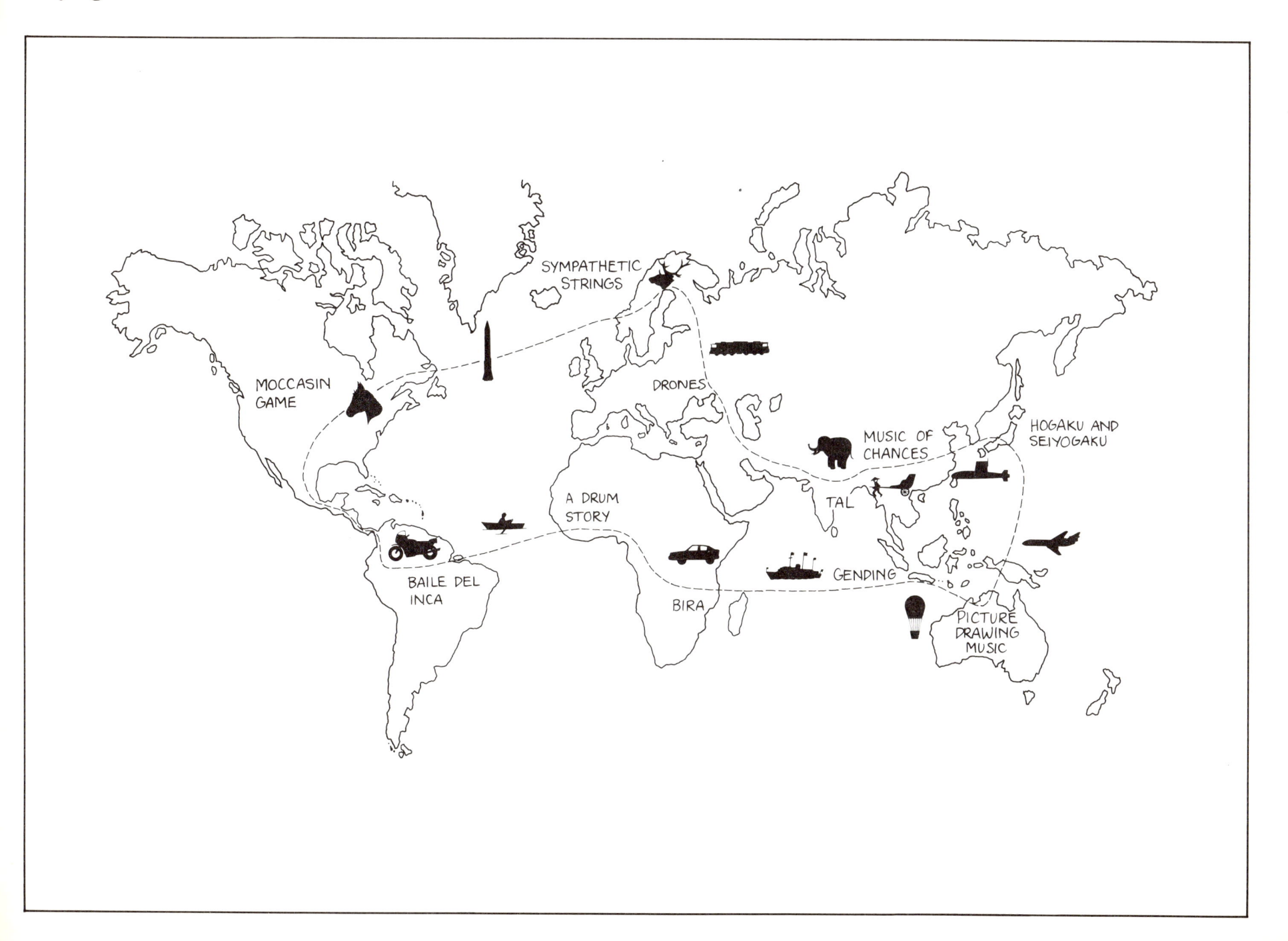

63

Useful addresses

Pitt Rivers Museum,
Dept. of Ethnology and Prehistory,
University of Oxford,
South Parks Road,
Oxford OX1 3PP.

Museum of Archaeology and Anthropology,
University of Cambridge,
Downing Street,
Cambridge CB2 3DZ.

Ipswich Museum,
High Street,
Ipswich IP1 3QH.

British Museum,
Museum of Mankind,
6, Burlington Gardens,
London W1.

Victoria and Albert Museum,
Cromwell Road,
London SW1.

Horniman Museum,
London Road,
Forest Hill,
London SE23 3PQ.

Commonwealth Institute,
Kensington High Street,
London W8 6NQ.

Cambridge Anthropology Sound Archive,
Rivers Research Laboratory,
Dept. of Social Anthropology,
Free School Lane,
Cambridge CB2 3RF.

Ethnomusicological Audio-Visual Archive,
Centre of Music Studies,
School of Oriental and African Studies,
University of London,
Malet Street,
London WC1E 7HP.

Topic Records Ltd.,
50, Stroud Green Road,
London N4 3EF.

Tangent Records Ltd.,
176a, Holland Road,
London W14 8AH.

Lyrichord Records,
141, Perry Street,
New York, N.Y. 10014,
U.S.A.

Nonesuch Records,
665, Fifth Avenue,
New York, N.Y. 10022,
U.S.A.

Sussex Publications Ltd.,
Townsend,
Poulshot,
Devizes,
Wiltshire SN10 1SD.